"Mindfulness has been shown to reduce anxiety, depression, and anger; increase the frequency of positive emotions; speed physical healing; and increase the attention of students with attentional difficulties. It is a skill that everyone should have in their toolbox. Cook-Cottone and Vujnovic have done much-needed work to put mindfulness skills into age-appropriate and meaningful language for anxious children. With their work, it is my hope that we can teach a generation of children to be more mindful, calmer, and less anxious."

—**John Schinnerer**, high-performance coach, consultant to Pixar's *Inside Out*, and author of *How Can I Be Happy?*

"This book is a treasure trove of practical and powerful skills for kids to manage stress and anxiety, and for adults who love kids to teach and to model in their own lives."

—**Dzung X. Vo, MD, FAAP**, author of *The Mindful Teen*

"This book takes kids by the hand and leads them gently and lovingly to an experience of self-awareness. Through progressive exercises, each building upon the last, children learn to honor their own feelings and trust in their capacity to address challenges great and small. I can hardly wait to share this wonderful resource with my own students!"

—**Louise Goldberg, MA, C-IAYT**, founder of Creative Relaxation®, owner of Yoga Center of Deerfield Beach, author of *Classroom Yoga Breaks* and *Yoga Therapy for Children with Autism and Special Needs*, and coauthor of *S.T.O.P. and Relax*

S0-AED-101

"*Mindfulness for Anxious Kids* is so much more than a workbook, it's a step-by-step, trauma-informed framework for introducing mindfulness to children while empowering them with critical coping skills. Using the engaging self-images of Stressed-Out Me and Mindful Me, Cook-Cottone and Vujnovic first teach about stress and anxiety and how our bodies and brains work together to manage them. The reader is then artfully guided in strengthening their Mindful Me through powerful, effective, age-appropriate skill-building activities, including some designed to specifically address stressful situations common to children. This brilliant resource belongs at the very top of the toolbox of every parent, clinician, counselor, and anyone else who supports the emotional well-being of children!"

> —**Lisa Flynn, E-RYT 500**, founder and CEO of ChildLight Yoga and Yoga 4 Classrooms, and author of *Yoga for Children, Yoga 4 Classrooms Activity Card Deck*, and *Yoga for Children—Yoga Cards*

"For the children who feel like their body and mind betray them, this book will be a true gift, allowing them to explore, understand, and grow a trust for the inner resources we all deserve to know. The way *Mindfulness for Anxious Kids* is organized makes complete sense; it progressively moves children through cultivating self-awareness to developing effective ways to manage what they discover about themselves. When children engage with this workbook, they'll be empowered to choose their best self, more often. More importantly, they'll practice uncovering what blocks them from being comfortable with who they are."

> —**Kelli Love, MEd**, is an educator and consultant in the field of mindfulness in education. She created the short film, *Aliza and the Mind Jar*.

"This workbook is a treasure! Through a series of practical and engaging activities, children learn about what anxiety looks and feels like in Stressed-Out Me. Children also get to know their Mindful Me and practice core tools of mindfulness. Many examples are provided so that children can apply these skills to manage anxiety, perfectionism, and everyday stress in different situations, such as tests, social situations, and emergency drills. With the prevalence of anxiety in youth, this book is a must for children, teachers, clinicians, and parents."

> —**Amanda Nickerson, PhD**, professor in the department of school psychology and director of the Alberti Center for Bullying Abuse Prevention at the University at Buffalo, State University of New York; and coauthor of *School Crisis Prevention and Intervention*

"Statistics indicate that anxiety is rising both in adults and children; kids are noticing the anxiety in their adults' lives. *Mindfulness for Anxious Kids* is a really important book because it helps young readers both identify and address their worries. This practical guide teaches kids to root themselves in breathing; it actually provides action guides. From the get-go the book instructs children to ask for support when they notice stress. The book teaches them how and where stress resides in the body, and provides relaxation tools to help them disconnect from the stress. The authors adeptly teach children how to get out of their heads to 'be right here right now.' They even describe a lovely worry tree where kids can leave their worries and then pick them up again when they are prepared to deal with them. I would keep this gem in the medicine cabinet."

> —**Laurie Grossman**, director of social justice and educational equity at Inner Explorer, Inc., and cofounder of Mindful Schools

Mindfulness for Anxious Kids

A Workbook to Help Children Cope with Anxiety, Stress & Worry

CATHERINE COOK-COTTONE, PhD
REBECCA K. VUJNOVIC, PhD

Instant Help Books
An Imprint of New Harbinger Publications, Inc.

Distributed in Canada by Raincoast Books

Copyright © 2018 by Catherine Cook-Cottone and Rebecca K. Vujnovic
      Instant Help Books
      An imprint of New Harbinger Publications, Inc.
      5674 Shattuck Avenue
      Oakland, CA 94609
      www.newharbinger.com

Cover photograph is a model used for illustrative purposes only.

Cover design by Amy Shoup

Mindful Me illustration on page 28 by Oliver Burns

Acquired by Elizabeth Hollis-Hansen

Edited by Karen Schader

Library of Congress Cataloging-in-Publication Data on file

20   19   18

10   9   8   7   6   5   4   3   2   1   First Printing

To mindfulness and yoga and all they have taught me in my life.

To all the hours spent practicing, and all the times that I felt uncomfortable, got lost in my thoughts, and forgot my center and my own body. Although difficult, these times have been great teachers.

To all the moments I remembered and found my breath, my center, and my own body. These are the moments when I have been my best self, my Mindful Me.

To my Mindful Me; you do a lot of good. It is for these reasons, from deep within my own practice and my own experience, that I wanted to write this book, so that some day, all the kids who work through it will have access to their best selves, their Mindful Me.

To my husband, Jerry Cottone, and my two kind, smart, and beautiful daughters, Chloe and Maya Cottone, who believe in me and my work and love me even when I am writing a book (with a lot of grounded, deep breaths—of course).

And to Rebecca. I have known her since she was a student at the University at Buffalo. I recall our talks in my office when we wondered together about how to best help kids cope with family and other challenges. She stood out way back then. She is now my colleague and someone I am truly blessed to know. I am so happy for this project and a chance to create together.

—Catherine Cook-Cottone

To my own children, Audrianna, Cole, and Cullen, and the many others I have had the privilege to work with along the way. You have, collectively, been the most influential teachers.

To Michael, for being my person. Thank you for being with me on this incredible and unpredictable journey.

And to Catherine, for your friendship, mentorship, and incredible wisdom. Thank you for this opportunity.

—Rebecca Vujnovic

Contents

Section 1: What Makes You Anxious and Stressed Out?

Section 2: Getting to Know Your Mindful Me

Section 3: Your Mindful Me in Action

Foreword

Thank you for choosing this book for your anxious child—and for yourself. I know that parenting an anxious child can be a challenge, but you'll find so much helpful advice in these pages for understanding anxiety, stress, and mindfulness as you explore these activities alongside your child.

As you begin this journey together, you'll get to know your child's *Stressed-Out Me* and *Mindful Me*. Catherine and Rebecca (Doctors Cook-Cottone and Vujnovic) have created these alter egos to help anxious children identify and work with their challenges to become their *best* selves. When a child (or a parent, for that matter) practices the fun mindfulness exercises in this book, their *Stressed-Out Me* will be far less likely to show up in their life. And as a child gets to know when and where their *Stressed-Out Me* tends to show up, they learn to manage those moments with mindfulness, instead of becoming overwhelmed by stress and anxiety.

A *Mindful Me* lives in every child too, ready to help when things get too stressful. The *Mindful Me* uses seven pieces of wisdom and lots of fun and helpful mindfulness tools that help kids manage even the most stressful situations. Over time, and with practice, your child will learn to find and connect with their *Mindful Me* even in moments when you (or this book) are not right there to help.

Learning that mindfulness is available to them at *any moment*, and internalizing mindfulness skills, allows kids to thrive as they grow. Once they have practiced and mastered the skills, the lessons of this book can go anywhere that kids and their stress go. What's more, these skills will grow along with your child, helping them find their *Mindful Me* wherever it's needed—from the school play to the soccer sidelines, and to middle school, high school, and beyond.

There is just as much in these pages for you as there is for the anxious child in your life. One of the best things this book offers is a way to bring the two of you closer as you work on it together, practicing the exercises and learning a common language for discussing stress, anxiety, and mindfulness. And you may learn a bit along the way about how to manage your own stress and anxiety—which will be a gift for both you and your child. Better than any strategy or idea you can offer a kid is your calm, compassionate, and—most of all—*present* self.

I wish you and your child much health and happiness—and a lot less stress and worry—in the years ahead.

—Christopher Willard, PsyD, author of *Growing Up Mindful and Raising Resilience*; faculty at Harvard Medical School

An Introduction for Clinicians

Welcome to *Mindfulness for Anxious Kids*, a workbook that gives kids ages seven to twelve effective, mindfulness-based tools to manage anxiety and stress. Through each activity, kids practice being their own Mindful Me—the part of themselves who has the mindfulness skills to handle life's stresses. The Mindful Me gives kids powerful tools for coping with big and little stressors at home, at school, and in relationships. When a child has these tools, stress and anxiety no longer overwhelm.

This workbook helps by focusing on skill building. Children create a sense of inner ease and competency as they learn to calm themselves and tolerate anxiety and distress as it arises from both inside and out—that is, they learn to cope. Mindful Me tools engage the child's body, feelings, and thoughts. With practice, the Mindful Me tools presented in this workbook help kids feel less stressed and anxious, and more empowered, safer, and happier.

The Mindful Me is a self-image that knows what to do to combat stress and anxiety. A child who is identified with the Mindful Me is able to access seven key modes of intentional, mindful action, each paired with an "I" action guide:

1. present-moment awareness: *I am right here, right now.*

2. bare attention: *I am mindfully aware inside and out.*

3. focus of attention: *I can choose and maintain my focus.*

4. curiosity/release of judgment: *I am curious. I can try.*

5. distress tolerance: *I use my mindfulness tools to cope.*

6. intentional action: *I choose my actions on purpose.*

7. heartfulness: *I am kind and caring to myself and others.*

This book is organized in three sections:

What Makes You Anxious and Stressed Out?, activities 1 through 7, starts with teaching two powerful skills that work well together: grounding and calming breaths. Kids meet the Stressed-Out Me, a self-image that is easily overwhelmed and reactive. They learn about anxiety and stress and how they feel in the body, and how they may be triggered and stressed.

Getting to Know Your Mindful Me, activities 8 through 15, teaches kids about mindfulness and how mindfulness skills can help with worries and stressors. In this section, kids practice the core tools of mindfulness, such as attention training, focusing on the senses, and observing thoughts and feelings. They also learn about being open-minded and openhearted through curiosity and being accepting about people and things.

Your Mindful Me in Action, activities 16 through 30, teaches kids how to create their own peaceful places, ride the waves of emotions, and create mindfully at home. They also learn how to be mindful friends through listening and showing compassion. Importantly, kids consider what it feels like to be with a good friend so that they can choose their friends mindfully. School skills include mindfulness tools for test anxiety, feeling stuck, stressful situations, and missing your parents. This section also teaches how to let worries go and cope with sudden panic. Kids also practice gratitude for all the work they did in completing this workbook and review all the skills they learned.

Supporting materials for some of these activities can be downloaded at http://www. newharbinger.com/41313. (See the back of this book for more details.) Following activities 1 through 30, you'll find two additional activities intended to support children in handling trauma and large stressors.

Mindfulness for Anxious Kids is designed to help children broaden and build a body of skills, including empirically supported mindfulness techniques, that will help them successfully manage anxiety and stress. We intend it to be helpful for counselors, teachers, and other professionals who work with children, as well as parents. It is designed to be accessible, with activities that are easy to understand and use. Further, even though these activities are certainly helpful for children who are struggling with anxiety and stress, this workbook can be used to help a range of children managing everyday events that might create stress.

A Note for Parents

Dear Parent,

It can be very challenging to support children who are sensitive to stress, or experience anxiety, or have lived through trauma. Even ordinary events or situations can seem bigger and more difficult for them. There are many ways to support your child's ability to cope with and manage stress and anxiety, and this workbook is full of them.

Mindfulness for Anxious Kids includes thirty activities that promote mindfulness and calm in the face of worry and stress. Supporting materials for some of these activities can be downloaded at http://www.newharbinger.com/41313. (See the back of this book for more details.)

Throughout the book, the child gets to know and identify with his own Mindful Me—a part of himself that knows how to handle worrisome situations. We also meet the Mindful Me's counterpart, the Stressed-Out Me, who feels and acts quickly—sometimes with not great results, especially when fear and anxiety are involved. These characters can be helpful tools for your child—and they can also help you help him. When life events or feelings seem too big for your child, you might say, "I wonder what your Stressed-Out Me might do right now. What do you think your Mindful Me might decide to do instead?"

The mindfulness activities build on one another. We'll start by learning what anxiety and stress are, and how our brains and bodies work together to manage them. The first group of activities in the book will have your child thinking about and listing the things that worry her or make her anxious. Because this can be pretty heavy stuff, the very first two activities give her some tools that will help her cope with these explorations: basic techniques for grounding and breathing, and an activity that will teach her how and when to ask for help.

In the next section, your child meets Mindful Me and learns about mindfulness and how mindfulness skills can help with worries and stressors at home, with friends, in school, and in dealing with various problems. Your child will practice the core tools of mindfulness, such as how to pay attention, focus on the five senses, and observe thoughts and feelings without reacting. Your child will also learn about being open-minded and openhearted by practicing skills that develop curiosity and compassion.

The final section of the book includes problem-solving activities that address specific struggles like handling big feelings, focusing attention, feeling lonely, letting go of worries, sleeping, and coping with panic. If your child has a history of trauma, there is an additional activity at the back of the book to help her understand what trauma is, and an activity designed to help her ask for help with the overwhelming thoughts and feelings that can arise.

You may find some of these activities useful in your own life. One of the most powerful things a parent can do is to model the skills and ways of being they would like to see in their children. A favorite motto of ours is "You can't give what you don't have," which means that it is difficult to offer mindfulness and calm to your child if you do not practice it yourself. We encourage you to practice alongside your child and bring even more mindfulness and calm into your home.

We believe that the spirit in which you undertake this work with your child can make all the difference. Learning to approach stress and worry in a mindful way takes time, perseverance, and a lot of practice. There are practical considerations, too. Some kids like to work on their own, and parent support can be offered through Mindful Me check-ins. Other kids thrive with one-on-one workbook time with a parent, with a scheduled Mindful Me time each week. Offer support and help and then let your child take the lead. The old saying is still true—the way we learn something can be just as important as what we learn. Bring your own Mindful Me to the process.

If you feel like you and your child need more support, we encourage you to reach out to a counselor in your child's school or in your community. It can be helpful to bring this book so the counselor can work though the activities together with your child, or with both you and your child.

We are excited for you as you begin your journey exploring the effectiveness and experiences of learning these mindfulness practices with your child.

Best,

Catherine and Rebecca

A Note for Kids

Welcome to *Mindfulness for Anxious Kids*. If you are reading this book, it means you are looking for ways to feel less stressed. All kids are stressed sometimes, but feeling too stressed or anxious too much of the time can make you pretty unhappy. It doesn't have to be like that! This book is here to help.

In this book you will learn about two parts of yourself: Mindful Me and Stressed-Out Me. Stressed-Out Me gets upset easily and worries a lot. Mindful Me knows how to handle big feelings and has a bunch of tools that help you feel calm and strong. Everyone has a Mindful Me and a Stressed-Out Me inside them. And everyone—even kids—can learn to make their Mindful Me stronger.

This book will help you learn about anxiety and stress, and how your brain and your body can work together to help you calm down and relax when you are getting stressed. You will learn tools you can use at home, in school, and when you are with other people.

Learning how to use your new mindfulness skills on your own is great. There might also be times when you want to talk to an adult who cares about you—maybe a parent or a teacher or counselor. You can do this at any time as you try your new skills. And you can use your workbook to show grown-ups you trust what you are working on and what is happening with your feelings.

Take your time and enjoy each activity. Move on to the next one whenever you feel ready. And ask for help when you need it. It can be hard to learn new things, but with practice, you'll get it. Good luck and have fun!

Warm wishes,

Catherine and Rebecca

Section 1

What Makes You Anxious and Stressed Out?

Stress. Worry. Anxiety. In this first part of the workbook, we'll talk about what those words mean. And we'll explore how worry, anxiety, and stress feel in your body and how they affect what you think and what you do.

Your brain and your body work together better when you are calm and not stressed than when you are stressed and worried. And you can learn to help your brain and body calm down and feel better.

Thinking about stress can be stressful! So we'll start with three things you can do anytime you start stressing about stressing. One is called grounding and the second is called calming breaths; these work very well together. You can do one of them or both of them, anytime and anyplace. They are easy and awesome, and you'll learn them right away and use them a lot.

The other thing we'll learn and practice together is asking for help. Grown-ups who care about you want to be on your team—they want to help! Sometimes it's hard to ask because you feel bad or just plain old stressed, or you don't know exactly what you need. Throughout the book, we'll see how other kids have asked their adults for help with their worry and stress. You can ask for help too. It is always, always okay.

Stress-Busting Basics
Grounding and Calming Breaths

For You to Know

Worries and stress and anxiety can feel uncomfortable in your body. You can also use your body to feel better right away. In this activity, you'll learn two great tools for feeling calmer: (1) grounding and (2) calming breaths. Here's how they work for a kid named Maya.

When Maya feels worried, she notices that her heart beats fast. She feels sweaty and struggles to focus on what people are saying. She sometimes feels shaky in her body. Her brain starts thinking of scary things and feels like it is going too fast.

As soon as she feels this happening, Maya stops what she is doing and does grounding. She stands still and presses her feet into the floor. She notices her feet—her heels, her toes, her socks, and her shoes—and focuses all her attention on feeling her feet press into the floor. She pretends she is a tall tree with deep roots growing into the ground and a loooooooong tree-trunk body that can bend in the wind without breaking.

Then Maya carefully does four slow calming breaths. She breathes in for one count and thinks, "I breathe in for one count … one." Then, she breathes out for two counts and thinks, "I breathe out for two counts … one … two." She does this slowly and deeply three more times. When she is done, her brain and body feel calmer.

Mindfulness for Anxious Kids

For You to Do

Now it's time for you to practice grounding and calming breaths. (You can ask a grown-up to read the instructions to you while you practice.)

1. Stand still and close your eyes. Notice how your body feels.

2. Press your feet into the floor. Notice your feet, your socks, your shoes as you press into the floor. Imagine that you are a tall tree with deep roots. You are strong and also soft and relaxed, so that you can bend in the wind if it blows, and you can also be still. You are doing grounding.

3. Now focus on your breath. Breathe in slowly, saying to yourself, "I am breathing in for one count ... one." Breathe out, saying to yourself, "I am breathing out for two counts ... one ... two." Make sure you breathe out twice as long as you breathe in. Do this four times: Breathe in one; breathe out one, two. You are doing calming breaths.

4. Take a minute to notice your body now. Your heartbeat may feel slower. Your body may feel softer and more relaxed. Your thinking may be clearer. What do you notice?

Grounding and calming breaths work best when you practice. You can practice each day right after you brush your teeth or while you wait for the bus. They are great to practice while you are waiting for your parents to pick you up. The more you practice, the better.

More to Do

Next time you do this, when you breathe in, lift your heart and the top of your head up toward the sun (just like a tree grows toward the sun), and when you breathe out for two counts, press your feet into the earth like the roots on a tree. This is the advanced level grounding and calming breaths practice! Do this practice for four deep breaths in a row, too.

Remember, you can use either of these practices when you do the activities in the book, especially the ones that get you thinking about your worries.

Help Is on the Way!

For You to Know

It is okay to ask for help. Kids get help all the time for lots of reasons. You can ask for help when trying to reach something that is too high up. You can get help in math or to get better at soccer. You can also get help with feelings.

Sandro told his soccer coach that he would be at the game on Saturday. The very next day, Eric asked Sandro if he wanted to go to the beach with his family. Sandro said, "Yes!" He was super excited until he realized that he had already promised he would be at the soccer game. Then he was worried. His coach and Eric were both going to be mad. He was stuck. He was afraid to talk to them and did not know what to say.

Sandro told his dad, "Dad, I made plans with Eric at the same time as the game. I'm afraid they will be mad at me. I don't know what to do." Sandro's dad smiled and sat down, and together they practiced grounding and calming breaths. When Sandro felt calmer, they talked and figured out what Sandro wanted to do.

For You to Do

First, remember that it is always okay to ask for help!

Next, ask yourself these questions:

Do I know what to do?

Do I know how to do it?

Should I do it by myself?

If you answer no to any of those questions, it's time to ask for help. Think about who you could ask. Then, choose a person you trust and who will know how to help you. Ask the person for help by saying:

Can you help me? I don't know what to do about _____.

Can you help me? I don't know how to _____.

Can you help me? I don't think I should do _____ by myself.

If none of these questions feels quite right, you can say, "I need to talk. I think I might need help with something." Your person can help you figure that out, too.

More to Do

You can practice asking for help with your parents. Together, you can figure out who might be the best people to ask for help for the things you need help with. With your parents, make a list of these people. It can be good to keep copies of this list in your room and in your desk at school.

You can also ask your parents to tell you stories about times when they felt stuck and asked for help. Those can be some of the best stories.

Activity 3 What Stresses Kids Out?

For You to Know

It can be helpful to understand stress, worry, anxiety, and being scared and to learn the differences between all these things.

First, *stress* is mostly about everyday stuff—only the stuff is too much, too fast, too many things all at once, too loud, all with not enough resting time. After a while, with too much stuff going on and no breaks, even good things can stress you out.

Worry and *anxiety* can happen when you are stressed out. Worry and anxiety are a little like being afraid or scared, only when you are afraid, there is typically something *right there* that scares you, like a big, mean, growling dog! Being *scared* has to do with needing to be safe—right now. When you are worried or anxious, it is a bit different. The mean dog isn't right there. You *are* safe, though you might not *feel* safe.

Being worried or anxious is like being scared about something that *might* happen. Your body can feel a lot like it does when it is scared. Your belly might feel funny. Your heart might beat fast, and you might feel your muscles getting tight. You might get sweaty, hot, or shaky. Your brain might be imagining a lot of scary things. Even though the thing is not right there or happening right now, you keep thinking about it. That is *worry* and *anxiety*: feeling scared about something that is not happening now, and worrying how you'll be safe if it *does* happen.

Kayla worries that a tornado will sweep her house away just like in the movies. When Kayla thinks about it, she knows she is safe. There has never been a tornado where she lives.

Kayla didn't tell anyone about her worries for a long time. She thought her parents might think she was silly. Her worries got so big that she was having trouble sleeping. At school she was tired and her teacher was noticing. Kayla realized that she needed to tell her parents so she could get help.

Bravely, Kayla told her mom, "I've been having a hard time sleeping. I keep worrying that a tornado is going to come and take all of us away."

Her mom said, "Oh, Kayla, when I was little I worried about things like that, too. Lots of us have worries. There are many ways to handle worries. Do you want to learn some of them?"

Kayla hugged her mom and said, "Yes!"

For You to Do

Most kids, like Kayla, have some kind of stress, worry, or anxiety, and that's okay. Do you have stress, worry, or anxiety? Let's find out.

Here are some things that kids stress, worry, and get anxious about. You can add your own if they are not here.

Stresses	Worries and Anxieties
Too much work	Being liked
Having homework on vacation	Being perfect
Too many sports practices	Thunderstorms, earthquakes, tornadoes
A lot of afterschool activities	Monsters
Lots of activities	Mean kids
Arguing with friends	Being apart from my parents
Making everyone happy	Fires
Lots of tests	Mean grown-ups
Teachers liking me	Emergencies
Chores	People fighting
No time to rest	My parents fighting
Needing to catch up	Animals or people dying
Not enough help	People being sick
My mom or dad's stress	The news on TV
My sisters or brothers	My brother or sister being mean
Trying to get good grades	Not doing well enough
Too many things to do	Being picked on

_____   _____

_____   _____

_____   _____

More to Do

Share this activity with a helpful grown-up. Together, decide if you need help in figuring out how to get support now and which stresses and worries you can work on over time. You can practice your grounding and calming breaths right now as you work on asking for help.

When you and your grown-up have agreed on what help you can get, fill it in here:

When I feel stressed or worried about _____,

I can get help by _____.

If you want to, use the rest of this page to write about how you could get help when you have one of your big worries or stresses. And just so you know—the rest of this book is full of ideas and tools for you to use whenever you need help with worry.

_____

_____

_____

_____

What Do Stress and Anxiety Feel Like in Your Body?

For You to Know

Stress and anxiety are things you think about. They are also things you feel in your body. In fact, your body can help you know when you are having feelings of stress or anxiety. Once you know that these feelings are there, you can do lots of different things to feel better. The first step is knowing that the feelings are there. Your body can be a big helper here!

Eric was really worried about being called on to read in front of the class. His body felt funny, too—all jumpy and his belly felt bad. As his turn got closer, Eric noticed that his chest felt different; his heart was pounding and the muscles in his chest felt tight. Most of all, he noticed that his breathing felt different. He was breathing faster, and his breaths were shorter. When Eric's turn to read came, he felt horrible, and he wished he were anywhere but where he was.

Activity 4 What Does Anxiety Feel Like In Your Body?

For You to Do

Here is a list of ways our bodies can feel when we are worried or anxious. Circle the way you feel when you are worried or anxious. If you're not sure how you feel, it helps to tune into your body. Put one hand on your belly and one hand over your heart, and try to notice what's going on there.

Belly	Chest	Arms and Legs	Other Body Parts
Upset	Fast heartbeat	Hands and feet feel cold	Headaches
Achy	Tight muscles	Hands feel sweaty	Trouble swallowing
Feeling like your stomach isn't working to digest food	Breathing fast	Hands feel shaky	Feeling dizzy
	Short breaths	Legs feel shaky	Sweaty
Gassy	Feeling like you can't breathe	Leg and arm muscles are tight	Shaky
Going to the bathroom too often or not often enough	Shoulders turned forward	_____	Trembly
	_____	_____	Tired
	_____	_____	Body feels strange
_____	_____		Skin rashes
_____	_____	_____	_____

Now, use your grounding and calming breaths to calm your body. If you'd like, share your list with a grown-up. It's a good idea to get support when you are feeling big feelings.

More to Do

Draw a stick figure or an outline of a body.

Color or mark your drawing with crayons, markers, or pencils to show the ways that anxiety and worry feel in your body. You can talk with your parent or another adult you trust about why you chose each color, or you could describe the things you think about when you feel these sensations in your body.

What Are Your Big Worries?

For You to Know

Doctors who study worries and stress tell us that writing our worries down can help us feel better. Everyone worries about different things. When you know what things worry or stress you, you can learn to handle them better. Taking a few minutes to write them down will help you know and remember what they are.

Sarah was worrying every day about lots of things. She worried about being in a car accident, her cat getting outside, leaving the water running in the shower, and her parents being safe. Sarah decided to talk to her school counselor. Together they wrote down all the things that were worrying Sarah. After they talked about each, Sarah circled the ones that worried her the most. She and her counselor talked a lot about those big worries. She felt better after telling her counselor and even better writing it all down.

For You to Do

Give it a try now—make a list of your worries in the space below. If you're not sure what to write, it might help to think about your day—waking up, getting ready for school, eating breakfast, going to school, seeing your teacher and friends, doing schoolwork, going to music, creating art, playing outside, going to lunch, playing after school, going to practice, heading home, seeing your parents, doing homework, being with your family, eating dinner, getting ready for bed, and going to bed. Think about the weekends, too—playing sports, seeing friends, doing homework or chores, being with family. As you think about the things you do, what worries come to your mind? For example:

1. Being in a car accident.

2. My cat might get outside.

3. Going to school.

If making this list makes you feel stress or worry in your body, stop for a minute and use grounding and calming breaths (from activity 1). When you feel better, keep going with the list.

4.

5.

6.

7.

8.

More to Do

Share your worry list with a grown-up. Talk about them. Together, circle your biggest worries or stresses, the ones that seem to really bother you. Now, put a star next to the *very biggest* ones. These big worries are a good place to start practicing ways to feel calmer. You already have these good ones: grounding, calming breaths, and asking for help. You'll learn more as you keep working in this workbook.

What Are Your Worry Triggers?

For You to Know

Worries often have what we call *triggers*. These are the things that get our worries going. Triggers can happen on the outside, like hearing something (maybe a loud noise), seeing something (maybe a spider), or even smelling something. They could happen on the inside, like having feelings, thoughts, or memories. When this happens, we call it *getting triggered*.

Joe does not like to ride the bus. He worries that the bus driver won't be able to stop or that the bus will tip over when they go around a sharp corner. His worries get really big when he is on the bus. But even when he is not on the bus, Joe worries about the bus.

Joe noticed that his worries get going when the announcements at school talk about the buses, or when he sees a bus out of the window, or even a picture of a bus in a book or on a bulletin board.

For You to Do

Turn back to the last activity and find the worries and stresses you circled and put stars next to. Then follow these steps:

1. In the first column, write down your list of big worries from that page.

2. Go through a day, or two days, and notice what's happening when your worries feel big.

3. In the second column, write all the triggers you notice. What was happening when your worries got going? Did you see, hear, feel, smell, or remember something? Maybe it was a picture or a sound. Maybe it was a person, place, or thing. Write them all down.

4. Draw lines between your triggers and the worries in the other column.

You can download a copy of this chart, called "My Worry Triggers," at http://www.newharbinger.com/41313 and keep this list of triggers, the things that get your worries going. You can add to it when you notice triggers you may have missed.

My big worries	My triggers
(Example: *Something happening to a parent*)	(Example: *Seeing my mom's writing on a note*)

More to Do

Try grouping your triggers together. Are there sounds, things you see, smells, things you remember, things people say, or a certain time, like before or after school? What do you notice about your triggers?

When you begin to feel your triggers or your worries starting to get going, you can use your grounding and calming breaths and say, "I am okay; that is just my trigger."

Sharing and teaching also helps worries settle down and can help you feel more relaxed and okay. If you have a favorite stuffed animal, you can teach it about your triggers and show it how to do grounding and calming breaths and say, "I am okay; that is just my trigger." You can also show an adult what you figured out. You can teach this adult how to ground and do calming breaths with you.

For You to Know

When people get upset or scared, there are three main ways they react:

- They get mad and feel like yelling or fighting.

- They find a way to run away or hide.

- They freeze up and can't think of what to do.

Everyone does one or more of these things when they get scared. And when we fight or run or freeze, our Stressed-Out Me is there. You can tell when your Stressed-Out Me is there—you might *feel* like fighting, arguing, leaving, quitting, or sleeping, or you might *feel* stuck. The Stressed-Out Me can be different for each kid, but basically, it's the part of your brain that *feels* afraid and is trying to do its best to save you. It's pretty cool that the *feeling* part of your brain jumps in right away to help you, but it's also true that this part of your brain doesn't always make the best choices. Not by itself. Sometimes when it thinks it's saving you, it's really just stressing you out.

When Jordan gets stressed or triggered, he feels mad. Pretty quickly, he gets into a fight. He says and does mean and angry things. This has not worked out for him, but he doesn't know what else to do when he feels like that. He has lost friends and gotten into a lot of trouble at school.

Jordan is working with his school psychologist to manage his anger and urges to fight. He has learned a lot about his brain. He learned that when the feeling part of his brain gets all worked up, the thinking part of his brain needs a little time to catch up. He learned how to slow down his feeling brain and give his thinking brain a chance to help him out. Two of his best tools are grounding and calming breaths, which he often uses together. When he is calmer, his feeling brain doesn't take over, he makes better choices, and he fights less.

For You to Do

When you get scared or super stressed, what does your Stressed-Out Me do? Write down one of the things that triggers you, then put a check mark to show how you react. Remember, the three stressed-out responses are: (1) fight, or feeling edgy, mad, and like fighting; (2) flight, or feeling like you want to run away or quit; and (3) freeze, or feeling stuck, like you can't do anything, or super sleepy when you think about the problem.

When _____ happens:

I get edgy and feel like fighting with my friends and the adults in my life.

☐ Not really   ☐ A little   ☐ Sometimes   ☐ A lot

I want to run away from the situation, or I think of ways I can quit.

☐ Not really   ☐ A little   ☐ Sometimes   ☐ A lot

I get stuck and feel like I can't do anything, or I get really tired and just want to sleep.

☐ Not really   ☐ A little   ☐ Sometimes   ☐ A lot

In the chart that follows, write down what it's like for you when your Stressed-Out Me is in charge. What do you think, feel, say, and do when you are triggered or stressed?

Things my Stressed-Out Me does	Things I feel and think	Things I say or do
Fight (I feel like fighting.)		
Flight (I feel like leaving or quitting.)		
Freeze (I feel stuck or too tired to try.)		

If you would like to see how your Stressed-Out Me handles some of your other triggers, you can fill out this checklist and chart for more of your triggers. Just print out another copy, called "My Triggers Checklist and Chart," from http://www .newharbinger.com/41313.

More to Do

What do you notice about your Stressed-Out Me chart? When you are stressed out, what sorts of feelings and thoughts come out? What kinds of things do you say or do?

After their Stressed-Out Me calms down, kids sometimes wish they had done something differently. Have you ever wished you said or did something differently when you calmed down? Write or draw here one thing you do when you are calm that is hard to do when you are reacting.

In the next section, you are going to learn how to help your Stressed-Out Me be calm. For now, use your grounding and calming breaths to settle the feeling part of your brain so that the thinking part can help out.

Section 2

Getting to Know Your Mindful Me

We just learned about your Stressed-Out Me, and how it's the feeling part of your brain that is trying to help you when you're stressed or scared. Your Stressed-Out Me doesn't always have the best tools for helping, though. Sometimes its tools, like fighting or freezing or running away, just make more trouble.

Now you'll start learning about your Mindful Me. Everyone has a Mindful Me who is much better than the Stressed-Out Me at helping when you are stressed or anxious. The Mindful Me has a lot of tools and skills. You've already learned two of them: grounding and calming breaths. When you practice your Mindful Me skills, your body and brain can help you be calm, happy, and brave.

Your Mindful Me's Action Guides

For You to Know

The Mindful Me is something all of us have inside. When it is strong, it notices when we are getting upset, helps us calm our stress and think more clearly, and lets us makes lots of good choices, even when things are stressful. Our Mindful Me knows seven things, and when we remember to tell ourselves those things, they help us worry less and have more fun. Here are the seven things:

1. I am right here, right now.

2. I am mindfully aware inside and out.

3. I can choose and maintain my focus.

4. I am curious. I can try.

5. I use my mindfulness tools to cope.

6. I choose my actions on purpose.

7. I am kind and caring to myself and others.

These seven things are called *action guides* because they remind us of the best ways to act. When we learn and practice them, we can use them when things get hard—when we need them the most. We'll learn what they mean and how to use them in the next few activities.

Devon's parents got divorced when he was in second grade. He visits his dad's house on the weekends. He does not like to leave his mom and worries about her the whole time he is with his dad. Also, when he is at his mom's, he thinks about his dad. Every day, he worries and stresses about his parents and where he is going to be. His Stressed-Out Me wants to help, but it only helps him feel frozen, and even more stressed.

At school, he is learning about how to be the Mindful Devon. Devon does his grounding and his calming breaths and says: "I am right here, right now." It quiets down Stressed-Out Devon because it reminds him that it's okay to be where he is right now. It helps him listen to the thinking part of his brain, which knows his mom and dad are also both okay.

Now whenever he feels his worries trying to get too loud, he finds a comfortable seat, presses his feet into the floor to do the grounding practice, puts his hands over his heart, and takes four calming breaths. Then, he says to himself four times, once with each breath: "I am right here, right now." "I am right here, right now." "I am right here, right now." "I am right here, right now." He's starting to get really good at letting his worries go and just being right where he is—with his mom, with his dad, or at school with his friends.

For You to Do

Think about a time when your worries made it hard for you to enjoy what you were doing. Look at activity 5, where you listed your worries, to remind you of some of the biggies. Write these biggies down here:

Now read these instructions all the way to the end so you know what to do. When you're sure you've got it, find a comfortable seat.

When you sit down, make sure your bottom is pressing into your chair and your feet are flat on the floor. Reach the very top of your head toward the ceiling as you press down into the chair. You are doing grounding, like you learned in activity 1, but in a chair. Feel how you are sitting calm and strong and steady, which is how your Mindful Me likes to sit.

Close your eyes and picture the time one of your worries made it hard for you to be happy just where you were. When you have that picture, or that memory, place your hands over your heart, one on top of the other, and feel your breath as you breathe in and out. Slowly, breathe in for one count, out for two counts. Then take four more breaths like this. With each breath, whisper inside your head, "I am right here, right now."

If you notice that you are thinking about your worries, or feeling them coming into your body, that's okay. Just keep breathing and thinking to yourself, "I am right here, right now."

When you are done, open your eyes, and stay right where you are for a minute. What do you feel like in your body? Notice your arms, legs, breathing, and heartbeats. Notice what is going on inside your belly and your head.

Write down or draw a picture of what you notice:

More to Do

Grounding and calming breaths and the reminder "I am right here, right now" might help you with other times when you are stressed out or worried. Try to remember to use these tools when you are stressed and notice afterward how you feel. To get ready, list three times when it might be good to use these tools.

1. _____

2. _____

3. _____

For You to Know

When you worry or feel anxious, it's hard to pay attention. When your teachers say, "Pay attention," what do they mean? Paying attention is not exactly the same as thinking. The first step to paying attention is noticing what's happening right here and right now. Next, you can use all your senses to notice what's happening, both inside yourself and outside. Your Mindful Me can use the action guide "I am mindfully aware inside and out" as you notice what you see, hear, smell, taste, and touch.

Jalen practiced by placing one hand on his belly and one hand over his heart. He whispered to himself, "I am mindfully aware inside and out." He listened for his own breath, breathing in and out. He listened for his own heartbeat, feeling the beat inside him, feeling his heart beat under his hand, and if he was very still, he could even hear his heartbeat in his ears. If his mind wandered, he brought it right back to the sounds in his own body. Next, with his eyes closed, Jalen noticed everything he could hear in his room. Once he was sure he had heard all he could hear in his room, he listened to the noises outside his room—the cars going by, the wind in the trees, and the birds chirping. Feeling better, he whispered to himself, "I am mindfully aware inside and out."

For You to Do

You can practice paying attention by first noticing and sensing what is right here, right now. Next, focus. If your mind wanders, bring it back to this moment and your focus. It can be fun to practice this with each of your senses:

- You can be mindfully aware with your eyes. Look through books on flowers, birds, or trees. Go to a museum or garden. Take a hike and see what you see.

- You can be mindfully aware with your nose. Bring all your focus to smelling something like soup, apple pie, or a flower. You can set up jars with things to smell, like cinnamon sticks or other spices, perfume on cotton balls, and cocoa powder.

- You can be mindfully aware with your ears. Focus on hearing by ringing a bell and noticing when the sound starts and ends. Sit quietly, and find the layers of sound from the outside to the inside of your room to the sound of your own breathing. Listen carefully to a song and notice all the instruments playing.

- You can be mindfully aware with your mouth. Try eating a raisin, a piece of chocolate, or an apple, being very aware. Focus on carefully and slowing tasting chocolate, a piece of fruit, or your sandwich.

- You can be mindfully aware with your hands. Cuddle your dog or pet your cat. Put together a box of different objects that all feel different: smooth rocks, rough rocks, felt, velvet, a small stuffed animal.

More to Do

Get an old shoebox to collect your tools for helping you practice attention. Add things to your box that will be fun to practice with. To practice attention to touch, you can add dried flowers, feathers, a seashell, or a stone. You can also keep a tiny stuffed animal in the box. To practice attention to smell, add a stick of cinnamon to sniff. To practice attention to sound, add a small chime or bell. For attention to sight, add pictures from magazines or photos of things you love. Colored pencils for drawing are great, too!

Now, if you feel stressed or worried, you can go to your box and practice bringing your awareness to each of your senses. As you practice, keep bringing your focus back to the object. Say to yourself, "I am mindfully aware inside and out." Breathe four calming breaths and repeat.

The Mindful Me loves to do this! The next activity will help you learn even more about mindful attention.

Activity 10

Practicing Attention with a Mind Jar

For You to Know

There are three steps to paying attention: (1) being present right here, right now, (2) noticing everything inside and out, and then (3) choosing what to pay attention to. First, you remind yourself, "I am right here, right now." Then you notice all the stuff on the *inside* of you. You can notice your feet, legs, belly, chest, arms, neck, face, and the very top of your head. You can notice yourself breathe in and out. You can also notice everything on the *outside* of you: the sounds and smells and things you see. Next, you can choose your focus.

Chloe worried about getting everything just right. She worried so much about being perfect that it actually caused her to make mistakes. Because she worried about what was going to happen, she could not focus her attention on what was happening right now. Chloe's teacher showed her how to practice seeing things differently, letting go of trying to get everything right. With her class, Chloe made what's called a mind jar. Then they all practiced noticing what was happening both inside and outside their bodies, and then focusing on their mind jars. Her teacher called this "paying attention." Practicing with her class and her mind jar, Chloe did not need to be perfect; all that mattered was that she tried. She loved this feeling.

For You to Do

A mind jar is something you can make with a few materials (and a helpful adult). First, let's make one, then we'll talk about how to use it.

You need:

- Empty clear water bottle, with a cap (use a plastic bottle, not a glass one).

- Water

- Liquid dish soap

- Clear glitter glue, glitter, and sequins (use different shapes, colors, and sizes).

- Duct tape and scissors to cut it

First, fill the bottle three-quarters full of water. Squeeze in a drop of dish soap, some glitter glue, and sequins. You can add extra glitter if you'd like. Screw on the bottle's cap as tight as you can (ask your adult helper to tighten it even more if you like). Wrap duct tape around the neck of the bottle and the top of the cap to make sure it won't leak.

Now you have your mind jar. How do you use it? Check in with your body, thoughts, and feelings and notice all around you (inside and out). Now:

1. Shake your mind jar, then hold it still or put it on the table.

2. Watch the pieces of glitter move around in the water, noticing and focusing on whichever pieces you choose. You will notice that sequins fall fast and glitter falls slowly. You can watch the swirls and whirls. Breathe and let your mind rest while you watch.

3. Say to yourself, "I can choose and maintain my focus."

4. Breathe four calming breaths and repeat, "I can choose and maintain my focus" with each one.

Your attention will wander sometimes. This is okay! When you notice that it has wandered, bring it back to the jar, and to your breath.

More to Do

You can use your mind jar in different ways. If you have Stressed-Out Me feelings and thoughts, place your jar on a table, press your feet into the floor, and breathe calming breaths (in for one count and out for two counts) until the very last piece of glitter has floated to the bottom of the jar. Keep bringing your focus back to the glitter. Say to yourself, "I can choose and maintain my focus."

You can also use your mind jar if you are nervous before a sports game or a test or something else that makes you anxious. You can use it to help calm down if you are mad at your parents or anyone else. If you use grounding, calming breaths, and your action guide "I can choose and maintain my focus," you can imagine and feel your brain calming down just like the glitter in the jar. The Mindful Me loves this activity.

Practicing Attention with the Sky Story

For You to Know

The Mindful Me action guide "I can choose and maintain my focus" can help you when big feelings are happening. To use your Mindful Me focus to notice thoughts and feelings without stressing about them, try a tool called the sky story.

When Daija feels sad, she thinks a lot of sad thoughts. Her sadness feels big. Sometimes she thinks she will never feel okay again. This makes her even sadder. Her mom told Daija that when this is happening to her, she can choose her focus and imagine that she is like the sky. The sky is always there; it is steady and safe. Feelings and thoughts are like clouds in the sky; they come and go. Daija can see the clouds come and go and keep her focus on the steadiness and safety of the sky. To help Daija imagine this, her mom recorded a sky story on Daija's tablet. When Daija feels sad and needs to remember that feelings and thoughts come and go, she breathes calming breaths, chooses her focus, and listens to the sky story. It helps her remember that she is okay.

For You to Do

To use a sky story like Daija does, start by recording it on a tablet or phone. You can read it yourself, or ask someone whose voice helps you feel steady and safe. Here's a sky story you can use, or you can write your own version in the space below. Read it slowly and pause a little after every line.

"Imagine that it's summer and you are lying down in the soft, warm grass by a beautiful tree, looking up at the sky. Imagine what the grass and the breeze might feel like. Imagine what the leaves, gently blowing in the breeze, might sound like. The sky is blue, and there are clouds moving slowly across the sky. Some are light and fluffy, and some are gray, dark, and stormy. You notice how the sky is like your mind, always there, steady and blue.

Pause here and breathe slow, calming breaths, in for one count and out for two counts. The sky is always there, steady and warm. Pause here and breathe four calming breaths, in for one count and out for two counts. You notice that some clouds are like thoughts. They might be happy thoughts, or worries. Still, the clouds come and the clouds go. You are there, steady, just like the sky and the sun. Pause here and breathe four more calming breaths, in for one count and out for two counts.

You notice some clouds are like feelings. Some are silly and you laugh, and some are heavy and sad and you cry. Choose your focus. You are not your feelings, just as the clouds are not the sky. They pass by, and you—the sky and the sun—stay, steady and warm. Bring your thoughts back to your breath. Pause here and breathe four calming breaths, in for one count and out for two counts."

Listen to your sky story when you feel stressed, sad, or lost in your worries. As you listen, keep bringing your focus back to the sky, noticing the clouds and your breathing. Say to yourself, "I can choose and maintain my focus." Breathe four calming breaths and repeat, "I can choose and maintain my focus."

More to Do

You can write and record your own calming story. Be sure to include these two things in your story: (1) something that is always there, like a river or the street in front of your house, and (2) two things that pass by, like leaves and fish in a river, or cars and trucks in front of your house. Now, you can write your story. You are the thing that is always there (a river or a street) and your thoughts and feelings are like the things that pass by, such as leaves and fish or cars and trucks. You can choose which things are thoughts (maybe the leaves or a car) and which things are more like feelings (maybe the fish or trucks). Then, tell yourself the story, recording it on a tablet or phone. Remind yourself that you are always there and the thoughts and feelings pass by, come and go.

For You to Know

"I can" and "I can't" are powerful words. When you say "I can," it means that you know how to do something *and* that you are able to do it. Sometimes when we say "I can," it's because we *know* we can do a thing. Sometimes when we say "I can't," it means we *think* we can't do it. But maybe we are just afraid to try. That is what happened to Kimberly.

Kimberly was learning lots of new things in math class, and it was hard. There was homework every day. Kimberly would get home, open her math book, and think, "I can't do this." Then she would sit tapping her pencil on her paper, feeling more and more stressed. She often pushed the math away and did other homework. Sometimes she even did her chores to avoid doing math. Each day she felt like she was getting more and more behind and the feeling of "I can't do this!" felt bigger.

Her counselor asked her to try something new. When Kimberly came home, she opened her math book and looked at the first question. Her counselor had asked her to say, "I am curious. I can try." Kimberly took four calming breaths, in for one count and out for two. She said, "I am curious. I can try." She began work on the first math problem. It was not easy. She had to look back at her notes to remember how to do it. Still, with her calming breaths and the reminder "I am curious. I can try," Kimberly finished her math homework. She did not put it off. She did not skip it. She felt good having made it through.

For You to Do

Let's find out how the difference between "I can't" and "I can" feels to you.

Find a friend (or a trusted adult) to try this activity with you. Stand facing each other a few steps apart. With your elbows bent, face your hands palms up. Ask your friend to place his or her hands on yours, palms down.

Now, as your friend tries to push your hands down, your job is to resist. Look at your friend and say, "I can't. I can't. I can't. I can't. I can't …" until you reach ten times. Release your hands.

How did that feel? Write or draw here:

Again, stand facing each other a few steps apart. With your elbows bent, face your hands palms up. Ask your friend to place his or her hands down on your palms again. Now, as your friend tries to push your hands down, your job is to resist. Look at your friend and say, "I can. I can. I can. I can. I can …" until you reach ten times. Release your hands. How did that feel? Was it different? Write or draw here:

More to Do

"I am curious. I can try" is something the Mindful Me knows. The Mindful Me looks at challenges with curiosity. Then the Mindful Me tries and finds out that "I can't" wasn't totally true after all. Another name for this is a *growth mind-set*. When you have a growth mind-set, you look at challenges and think, "How can this help me grow and learn?" instead of "This is probably going to be too hard."

Try the I can't/I can experiment with something you find challenging. It might be math, riding a skateboard, writing an essay, having a hard conversation, or doing a yoga pose. First notice what it feels like to say "I can't." Notice your body, emotions, and thoughts. As you try, keep saying "I can't." Write or draw what you noticed:

Try it again, taking four mindful breaths and saying "I am curious. I can try." Now try the activity and say, "I can, I can, I can, I can." Notice your body, emotions, and thoughts. Write or draw what you noticed:

Activity 13   Using Mindfulness Tools to Cope

For You to Know

Your Mindful Me can use mindfulness tools to cope. To *cope* means that you face stresses, worries, and big feelings without fighting, leaving, or freezing. Melissa used her mindfulness tools to cope.

Melissa has worries about being a great player on the lacrosse field. During lacrosse practice she feels safe and supported. It's easy to use her Mindful Me tools there. Still, during the game, her worries get very big. Her school counselor explained that it is in the game when she needs her tools the most. Melissa picked out the mindfulness tools she knew would work best on the field. Then, Melissa drew pictures of herself using the tools and imagined using her tools—over and over again. When she had two different pictures and had imagined herself coping more than twenty times, she was ready. The next game, as she went out on the field, she said, "I use my mindfulness tools to cope" and brought all that she had practiced with her onto the field.

For You to Do

Write down a time when it is hard for you to remember to use your Mindful Me tools.

It is hard for me to use my Mindful Me tools when: _____.

Now, like Melissa, choose one or two of your Mindful Me tools that you think will work best. Draw a picture of your Mindful Me using the tools when you need them most. Next, imagine yourself using the tools when you need them most—lots of times—until you feel ready.

More to Do

Try using your Mindful Me tools when you need them most. Doctors who have
studied coping tell us that sometimes it takes a lot of imagining and a bunch of tries.
Share with your parents or an adult you trust how your trying is going. You can
change your Mindful Me tools as you find the ones that work best. If you do, draw a
new set of pictures and imagine using each tool—lots of times.

For You to Know

It is important to know *why* you are doing something. For example, Sydney wants to be a good soccer player because she wants to support her teammates. Michael works to cope with his anxiety at nighttime so he can sleep better and be less cranky with his friends. Caleb studies because he hopes to be a dentist some day. They are following the Mindful Me action guide "I choose my actions on purpose."

Chandra loves her friends a lot. Yet, sometimes when she is anxious, stressed, or worried, she takes it out on her friends. When her worries get big, she yells, says hurtful things, and doesn't like to wait for her turn. She wants to work on her behavior. Why? Chandra wants to be a better friend, even when she is anxious. She decided to use her Mindful Me action guide "I choose my actions on purpose." The next time she was with her friends and started feeling anxious, she used her grounding and her calming breaths before she spoke or acted out so that she could be a better friend. When she was being more mindful, she yelled a lot less, did not say hurtful things much at all, and was able to wait her turn without being rude. This meant a lot to Chandra and her friends.

For You to Do

Your mindful whys are good reasons to do things differently. Here are some examples:

- ➲ To be a better friend

- ➲ To sleep better

- ➲ To have fewer stomachaches

- ➲ To feel calmer

- ➲ To show other kids they can be okay, too

- ➲ To hurt people's feelings less

- ➲ To get in less trouble

- ➲ To enjoy things more

- ➲ To enjoy my friends more

- ➲ To play my sport better

- ➲ To do better in school

- ➲ To get along with my parents better

Go back to activity 7 and look at the things your Stressed-Out Me does. Choose one of the things you would like to do differently.

My Stressed-Out Me does this: _____.

Write down your mindful whys for changing what you do.

➲ _____

➲ _____

➲ _____

➲ _____

➲ _____

➲ _____

➲ _____

➲ _____

➲ _____

➲ _____

➲ _____

More to Do

Sometimes Chandra forgets why it is so important to practice her Mindful Me tools. It helps her to remember her mindful why—that she wants to be a better friend. When she gets tired of practicing, she asks herself to do just a little more, for her friends, and that helps her keep going.

The next time you are struggling to practice your Mindful Me tools, look over your mindful whys and see if that will help you keep going for a bit longer. Some kids like to write their mindful whys down on note cards or in their planners to help stay on track. You can do this, too.

Practicing Heartfulness   Activity 15

For You to Know

Another thing your Mindful Me knows is that if you *do* something with kindness, you *feel* kind and caring. Being kind on purpose is sometimes called *heartfulness*. Heartfulness makes it easier to be kinder to yourself and to all the people in your life—even the difficult ones. It also makes it easier to use all the other Mindful Me tools.

Tukka often tried so hard to be perfect that she felt stressed and anxious. She said mean and critical things to herself, like "You can't do anything right" and "You always mess up!" She didn't realize it, but all the mean things she said to herself just added to her stress and anxiety. She learned about heartfulness from her counselor. Now, when she makes a mistake, she practices talking to herself like she would talk to a good friend.

She also practices heartfulness for her friends, her coach, and her teammates, and even with some of the kids she has a hard time with. Tukka has found that using heartfulness helps her feel much less stressed and anxious. Also, she sees that the less stressed she is, the better she does!

For You to Do

To bring more caring and kindness to what you do, practice saying three things about a person (including yourself):

1. One wonderful or beautiful thing about this person is …

2. I am thankful for this person because …

3. My positive wish for this person is …

In the box below, fill in the first column with the names of four people. Then fill in the second column about each person you listed. As you do this, use your grounding and your calming breaths.

Person	Heartfulness practice
Someone in your family that you love very much:	One wonderful or beautiful thing about this person is _____. I am thankful for this person because _____ _____. My positive wish for this person is _____ _____.

Someone you see every school day (for example, a teacher, coach, bus driver):	One wonderful or beautiful thing about this person is _____. I am thankful for this person because _____ _____. My positive wish for this person is _____ _____.
Someone you struggle to get along with:	One wonderful or beautiful thing about this person is _____. I am thankful for this person because _____ _____. My positive wish for this person is _____ _____.
You (yourself):	One wonderful or beautiful thing about this person is _____. I am thankful for this person because _____ _____. My positive wish for this person is _____ _____.

More to Do

The Mindful Me action guide for heartfulness is "I am kind and caring to myself and others." You can use it with parts of yourself or with experiences, as well as with people. Try using this action guide working with a feeling or a thought, such as a feeling or thought you have about your body. Try using it with something that happened in your day.

Still More to Do

You can even use heartfulness to send love and good wishes to people you don't know, but who are having a hard or scary time. Sharing kind wishes with others is a really good way to feel better and calmer.

1. Sit comfortably.

2. Place your hands on your heart and feel the warmth of your love.

3. Now, think about someone (or even a group of people) who might need your warm wishes.

4. Imagine your warm wishes, like a huge ray of sunshine, radiating out from you and reaching far away to that person (or group).

5. As you imagine sending your warmth, say, "May you be safe. May you be healthy. May you be filled with love." Repeat that as many times as you wish.

6. Take a few moments to sit quietly and feel the warmth of the love in your heart and feel the connection that sending your warm wishes brings.

Sending warm wishes to someone you don't know is a wonderful way to do something to help.

Section 3

Your Mindful Me in Action

In this section, you will learn how to use your new Mindful Me tools to help you feel better in many of the places you go every day. You will learn tools to use at home: tools like how to create a peaceful place, how to ride your roller coaster of emotions, and how being creative can help manage worries and anxiety. You'll learn to use your Mindful Me tools around your friends. Here, you will practice mindful listening and mindful speaking, compassionate practices, and how being around a good friend feels. Then you'll learn tools to help with test anxiety, feeling stuck, missing home, and managing stressful situations in school. Finally, you'll practice tools to use for solving bigger problems. You will create a calm-down kit, let go of worries, get to sleep, and practice thanks and gratitude for your learning in this workbook. You have done excellent work so far; here is your chance to practice your new Mindful Me skills in places you are likely to be every day.

Creating Your Peaceful Place

For You to Know

Sometimes, just being in a different place changes the way you feel. You might notice that you feel scared when you are at the doctor's office. In a different place, like a playground or park, you might notice that you feel happy because there are lots of fun things to do, and you feel safe or peaceful.

Ali's house is always loud and busy. As soon as Ali wakes up, he feels like he's caught in a whirlwind, getting ready for the day and rushing out to school. And once the bus drops him off at the end of the day, it's nonstop homework, dinner, and the constant noise of two sisters and a brother. Sometimes all this makes Ali feel anxious and overwhelmed.

Even though Ali shares a room with his brother, his bed is just his. It is his special safe place. Sometimes, when he feels overwhelmed, Ali goes up to his room, lies on his bed, pulls his big, heavy blanket on top of himself, closes his eyes, and feels the quiet safety of his special place. He uses the Mindful Me action guides "I am right here, right now" and "I use my mindfulness tools to cope."

For You to Do

Think about your house. Is there somewhere in your house that could be your own special place? It might be a room (like your bedroom) or a place inside a room (like a special chair or your bed). It might be a big space or a tiny space.

Describe your peaceful place:

Now list the things you would like to have with you in your special space to help you feel peaceful and calm. Things like a special blanket, a pillow, or a favorite stuffed animal might help the space feel peaceful and safe. Think about other ways to make the space feel peaceful. Could you hang a special photograph or drawing? What other things might you include in your peaceful place? Your peaceful place can be where you go when you need to feel calm and relaxed.

More to Do

In the space below, draw a picture of your peaceful place.

When you have finished, take a "picture" of your special place in your mind.
Then, no matter where you are, you can use that picture of your peaceful place.
Just close your eyes and imagine the feeling of being back there. If you like, use
one of the Mindful Me action guides, like "I am right here, right now" or "I use my
mindfulness tools to cope."

Riding the Roller Coaster Activity 17 of Feelings

For You to Know

Think of a roller coaster. The track goes up very high in some places and very low in other places, and it twists and turns. Sometimes the track has little bumps, and sometimes it's nice and flat. Feelings can be like that—sometimes calm and smooth, sometimes wild and bumpy.

No matter how it feels, though, a roller coaster is safe. The seat belt holds you in so that you can enjoy the ride without getting hurt. Learning to ride the roller coaster of your feelings is like putting on your seat belt and going along with the ride. It lets you feel curious about your feelings without being afraid they will hurt or overwhelm you.

Liam is terrified of dogs, and his grandma has a dog, a big one. Liam worries a lot about the dog hurting him, biting him, jumping on him, and scratching him. Liam doesn't like to go to his grandma's house because he worries so much about the dog.

This makes Liam sad, because he really loves his grandma. He likes to spend time with her, and she has such fun things to play with at her house. Liam knows that if he wants to have special time with his grandma, he needs to figure out a way to feel okay about the dog.

Liam decided to try thinking about his worry about the dog as a roller coaster. Where are the hills and low spots, and the bumps and smooth parts? At first, when he is getting ready to go to his grandma's house, when they get to her front door, and when he sees the dog for the first time, his worry feels huge. But usually, after a little while, his worry starts to go down. Liam's roller coaster around the dog is never completely calm and peaceful, but he knows that it doesn't always feel as huge as it does in the beginning of the visit.

For You to Do

Emotions can feel really big, even *huge*. But, when you learn to see your feelings as a roller coaster that goes up and comes down, you can learn to ride the roller coaster.

Think about a time when you had a very strong, not so nice, feeling. Write about what happened.

_____

_____

_____

What would you call your feeling?

_____

_____

Do you remember how your body felt when you were having this strong feeling? If so, describe it here.

_____

_____

As you remember your strong feeling, don't try to change it for yourself by trying to get rid of it or make it bigger. Just let yourself feel the way you feel, and breathe. Use your grounding and your calming breaths here to help you ride the wave. You might also use some Mindful Me action guides as you remember the feeling, like "I am right here, right now" and "I use my mindfulness tools to cope."

More to Do

If the strong feeling you just wrote about were actually a roller coaster, what would it look like? What's the part that's like going up the hill? What's the part that's like going over the top, or racing down, or speeding through a sharp turn? Draw the roller coaster here, and write in what each part is like:

At the very top of your roller coaster, what might you notice in your body, emotions, and thoughts that could warn you about the big hill of feelings that's coming?

Think about the Mindful Me tools you have learned so far. Which do you think might help you ride the wave of the emotion? Check which ones you might use:

- ☐ Grounding

- ☐ Calming breaths

- ☐ Paying attention with my five senses

- ☐ Mind jar

- ☐ Remembering my mindful why

- ☐ Heartfulness

- ☐ Being in my peaceful place

Mindfulness for Anxious Kids

Focusing Attention with Mindful Creating

For You to Know

It's hard to always pay attention to what is happening right now. And when we're worried, it can be *really* hard. This is because worries are all about things that aren't happening now. They are about things that happened in the past or might happen in the future.

The thing is, worrying about things we did before or about things that might happen doesn't help us in any way. Worrying only makes us worried! But paying attention to what is happening right now helps quiet that worry voice. A good way to have fun paying attention to what's happening right now is mindful creating.

Destiny worries a lot that something bad will happen to someone in her family. She worries that someone will get sick or have a heart attack, and she worries what might happen to her if that happens. When her worries are loud, Destiny notices that it is hard to do anything or to think about anything else.

Destiny has learned that she can choose to focus on something other than her worry voice. Destiny gets her favorite coloring book and her colored pencils. To help her focus, she says things like "I am picking up the green pencil, and I will use it to color the grass." "Now the grass is done, and I'm coloring this flower light purple." When she finishes, she takes a minute to look at her creation and see how she's feeling. She usually realizes that she is feeling much more relaxed, and that she's proud of what she made.

For You to Do

Gather everything you will need to color, like colored pencils and a coloring book, and maybe a pencil sharpener. Settle in someplace comfortable and do some grounding and calming breaths.

As you color, keep noticing what you are doing. Notice the color you choose to use first and what you choose to color with it. Tell yourself that there is no right or wrong way to color. This picture is your creation, and you can do it any way you like.

If you notice that your thoughts start to drift to other things, it's okay. Bring your attention back to your coloring. If you like, you can do what Destiny does: describing what you do as you do it. ("I'm using the light blue in the middle of this flower, and dark blue for the petals" or "I'm listening to the sound the pencil makes in the sharpener.") When you are finished, take a minute to think about how you are feeling now. Check in with your body. Do you feel more calm or more relaxed?

Below, write a few words or draw a picture about how you feel after doing mindful coloring.

You can do this activity when you are feeling worried, or when you aren't particularly worried. It's great for calming worry, but it's also just relaxing.

More to Do

There are so many ways to be creative. Circle the things that you like to do to be creative, and use the blank lines to add others:

Color	Do a craft	Play an instrument	Write a poem
Draw	Make jewelry	Practice a sport	Fold origami
Paint	Paint	Take pictures	Scrapbook
Sew	Do a crossword	Build with blocks	_____
Knit	Do a puzzle	Cook	_____
Crochet	Sing	Bake	_____
Embroider	Dance	Write a story	_____

Remember that you can choose to focus your attention here and now. Doing something creative is a really good way to practice this. Choosing to focus on the here and now helps quiet the worry voice.

Learning to Listen and Talk

For You to Know

Good friends are good listeners and kind talkers. When we listen mindfully to what our friends are saying, we listen to their actual words and also what they might be feeling while they talk. When our mind wanders away from what they're saying, we just bring it back to listening.

Justin learned about mindful listening and how it could make him a better friend. One day he was talking to his friend Jack, and he decided to practice it. Jack was so excited about his last soccer game and was telling Justin all about it—how good the other goalie was, how the coach was yelling, and how Jack was able to defend against one of the best players in the league. While Jack was talking, Justin listened. He did not think about what he was going to say. Once he found himself thinking about his own soccer game, and he noticed that he was not quite listening to Jack. He brought his attention right back to what Jack was saying.

When Jack was done, Justin said, "I heard you say that the other goalie was super good. Your coach was yelling at you guys like crazy. And you had a great game and defended against one of the best guys in the league, which is amazing. When I listen to you, I can tell why you love soccer!"

Justin discovered that when he didn't spend his time thinking about what he was going to say, or comparing Jack's game to one of his own, or thinking about something totally unrelated, he just enjoyed his friend's happiness. When Jack got to talk about one of his most exciting games, sharing it with a good listener and good friend, it made him feel closer to Justin.

For You to Do

Find a friend or a grown-up you trust and tell them that you would like to practice mindful listening with them. If they agree, ask them this: "Tell me about something that happened in the past few days that was important to you." Then listen while they talk, paying attention to their words and to their feelings about what they are saying. Every time you find yourself thinking about something different, just bring your mind back to what they are saying. When they're done, show that you were listening to both their words and their feelings by saying:

What I heard you say is … (Tell them what they said; you can use your own words.)

What I heard you feeling is … (Describe the feelings you believe they were having about what they were talking about.)

Since you're using this conversation to practice, ask them if you heard them right. It's okay if you weren't quite right, or if you didn't hear part of it. Good listening takes a lot of practice!

More to Do

Learning to listen mindfully is one important part of communicating like a good friend. Speaking mindfully and kindly is the other big part. When you talk to others, it's important to remember the Mindful Me action guides "I choose my actions on purpose" and "I am kind and caring to myself and others." You can practice thinking about what you are going to say before you say it, and saying it in a way that is kind and understanding.

To remember this, just remember to THINK. Ask yourself:

T: Is what I want to say **true**?

H: Is what I want to say **helpful?**

I: Am **I** the best one to say it?

N: Is it necessary to say it **now**?

K: Is it **kind** to this person, others, and myself?

If you can answer yes to all the THINK questions, then you can be sure that the message you are sending is worth it.

For You to Know

Compassion is a big and important word. It means that you notice when someone is having a hard time. It also means that you feel warmth or caring for that person and want to help. And it means you understand that everyone struggles sometimes, and that it's okay. Doctors who study anxiety and stress have figured out that feeling compassion makes us stress way less.

Sophia's friend Audrianna gets sick a lot, and sometimes she needs to go to the hospital. When Audrianna has to stay at the hospital, Sophia feels helpless. One night, Sophia told her mom that she wished there were something she could do to help Audrianna feel better. Her mom said that there was something they could do: they could send her warm, loving wishes. Sophia's mom showed her how to close her eyes and feel the warmth of the love in her heart. She sent Audrianna her warm thoughts, using the words of the loving-kindness meditation her mom taught her: "May you be safe. May you be healthy. May you be filled with love." It felt really good to do this, and Sophia realized that she wanted to send love to all the kids in the hospital. So she did. Her mom also told her that it's good to send kind wishes to ourselves also, and Sophia liked that too.

For You to Do

You can practice sending love and kind wishes to others and to yourself. Sit somewhere quiet and comfortable, do grounding and calming breaths, and try this meditation:

1. Sit comfortably.

2. Place your hands over your heart.

3. Think about a person you love. Feel the warmth of your love in your heart.

4. Send happy, loving wishes to that person. You can say, "May you be safe. May you be healthy. May you be filled with love."

5. Now think of other people you love, maybe other family members or friends.

6. Send happy, loving wishes to your friends and family by saying, "May you be safe. May you be healthy. May you be filled with love."

7. Send happy, loving wishes to yourself. Say, "May I be safe. May I be healthy. May I be filled with love."

8. Take a few moments to sit quietly and feel the warmth of the love in your heart.

More to Do

Sometimes it's easier to feel compassion for other people than it is to feel compassion and kindness for yourself. This is especially true when we think about something we wish we hadn't done, or think we should be doing something better than we are. You deserve kindness, even when you make mistakes. We all do. Learning to give yourself kindness, *no matter what*, is one of the best things you can do to have less worry, stress, and sadness.

Take a couple of calming breaths. Now think back to a time when you didn't feel good about something you did. Write about what happened.

_____

_____

_____

_____

Now write the thoughts you had about what happened.

_____

_____

_____

_____

You might notice that your thoughts were not kind. And you might think you should not have kind thoughts about what happened. But saying unkind things to yourself doesn't ever make things better. Most of the time, it actually makes things feel worse.

How you could have shown yourself kindness?

_____

_____

_____

_____

How would things have been different if you had been kind to yourself?

_____

_____

_____

_____

Using the loving-kindness meditation and showing compassion to others and yourself is a way to be gentle when things are hard, and to remind yourself that you can be kind to yourself and others.

Choosing Who to Spend Time With

For You to Know

A true friend is a person who helps you be your best self. One thing that means is that when you are with this person you notice you are more like your Mindful Me and less like your Stressed-Out Me. Sometimes being with someone makes us feel stressed out and anxious, even if that person is a friend. This is how it was for Lana.

Lana began to notice that when she was with her friend Kara, she felt a lot like her Stressed-Out Me—irritable, jumpy, and angry. Kara likes to borrow Lana's stuff and often doesn't return it or loses it. She doesn't listen to what Lana has to say. She asks Lana if she can copy her homework. It makes Lana upset. She noticed that her muscles are tense when Kara is around, and also when she thinks about telling Kara that she wants her stuff back, that Kara doesn't listen, and that she doesn't want Kara to copy her homework. Lana really likes Kara and sometimes they have fun, so all these feelings are confusing.

For You to Do

Like Lana, do you have a person you are not sure is a good friend? Think about that person, then answer these questions:

When I am with this person, am I more like the Mindful Me or the Stressed-Out Me? (check one)

☐ Mindful Me

☐ Stressed-Out Me

Does my body feel calm and safe when this person is around?

☐ Yes, I feel calm and safe.

☐ No, I feel extra anxious and stressed.

Are my feelings steady when this person is around?

☐ My feelings are steady when this person is around.

☐ My feelings are more like a roller coaster when this person is around.

Are my thoughts curious, kind, and creative, or do I get stuck in worries about what this person says and does?

☐ My thoughts are curious, kind, and creative when this person is around.

☐ When we're together, I get stuck in worries about what this person might say or do.

Does this person listen if I say how I am feeling? (If you are not sure, try it and see.)

☐   Yes, when I say how I am feeling, this person listens.

☐   No, I have tried and this person does not listen.

Does this person respect me if I set a limit (say no) or make a request (for example, stop doing that)? (If you are not sure, try it and see.)

☐   Yes, this person respects me when I set a limit or make a request.

☐   No, this person does not take no for an answer and keeps doing things even when I ask him or her to stop.

Am I being a good friend to this person?

☐   Yes, I work to be safe and steady, to listen and have fun, and to respect this person's requests and limits.

☐   No, I need to work on my own actions, too.

After answering these questions, write or draw what you are thinking and feeling about this friendship.

More to Do

Being mindful about your friendships will help you make choices. For example, you might decide to spend more or less time with the person. You might even need some help from a grown-up to figure it out. If you look ahead to the first bonus activity near the end of this book, you'll find feeling scales that can help you figure out if you need some support deciding what to do about your friendship. If you are feeling a lot of anxiety or a lot or numbness, it's a good idea to share how you are feeling with your parent or an adult you trust.

Planning Ahead to Deal with Stress

For You to Know

Events like taking a test, playing sports, or doing a performance can be stressful. Scientists have figured out that just a little stress can be good; it make you try harder to prepare by studying or practicing ahead of time. But having too much stress can actually make it hard to do your best work. So how can you make sure you have a little helpful stress, instead of a lot of unhelpful stress?

Amira doesn't like to take tests. She starts feeling nervous right when she gets on the school bus, and her stomach hurts. She gets so worried that when it's time to take the test, it seems like she has forgotten everything. She feels like she doesn't know any of the answers, which makes her worry even more. Her worry gets so big that she sometimes cries right there in class. Amira's counselor at school has helped her plan ahead for taking tests. With a plan in place, she knows what to do when she starts to feel worried. This makes her feel better about taking tests—she knows she can keep her worry from getting out of control.

For You to Do

Think about a test that you have coming up. (Although this section focuses on tests, you can take the same approach with other events, like concerts or games.)

What is the test? _____

What are you hoping will happen? _____

_____

How important is this outcome to you? _____

How confident do you feel about your ability to be successful? _____

The checklist that follows can help you get ready. You can download additional copies at http://www.newharbinger.com/41313.

The day before and morning of the test:

- ☐ Go to bed at your typical bedtime to get enough sleep.

- ☐ Eat a healthy breakfast.

- ☐ Make sure you have all the materials you will need (like pencils, paper, a calculator).

Which of these tools do you think you might use to help you keep calm?

- ☐ Grounding

- ☐ Calming breaths

- ☐ Focusing attention with the mind jar, sky story, or mindful creativity

- ☐ Practicing self-compassion

Use these lines to add other ideas.

_____

_____

_____

During the test:

Try to stay focused on the test. To stay mindful, you can use the tools you have learned before, like grounding and calming breaths, paying attention with your five senses, and practicing kindness to yourself.

If you start to feel nervous:

☐ Put down your pencil.

☐ Take a few deep breaths. Say, "I am breathing in … I am breathing out … I am breathing in … I am breathing out …" Do this three times.

☐ Next, say something positive and encouraging, like "I can do this."

Or, add your own encouragement here:

_____

_____

_____

More to Do

Sometimes even activities we love can feel stressful. Usually this happens when we have to perform somehow: playing in a sports game, dancing in a recital, singing or playing in a concert. One mindful coping tool to help with performance anxiety is to imagine how you would like the performance to go. Let's try it.

Describe a performance you have coming up that feels stressful:

_____

_____

Write about your worries about the performance (or draw about them if you'd rather):

How would you *like* the performance to go? Write about it or draw it here:

Now close your eyes, and imagine the positive performance above. Watch yourself do exactly what you hope you will. When you have a picture of a successful performance in your mind, it helps you feel more confident of your performance in the real situation.

When You're Feeling Stuck

For You to Know

As you learn more about your Stressed-Out Me and your Mindful Me, you'll start noticing when they show up. For example, when things feel really hard and you don't feel like you did your best, your Stressed-Out Me takes over. You might hear it saying negative things about you. The more we listen to our Stressed-Out Me's negative words, the more upset we can feel and the harder it can be to try our best. This is called getting stuck.

Every time Zah'Nayla has to do her homework, she always gets stuck. She feels like her mind goes blank, and she can't remember how to do anything. She starts hearing a voice telling her that she isn't smart, that she can't do it, and that she will get a terrible grade. That voice never helps her do her homework. Instead, it leaves her feeling more frustrated and stuck. When Zah'Nayla told her mom about her thoughts, her mom told her about ANTs (automatic negative thoughts). She told Zah'Nayla that those thoughts are just thoughts. Just because they're crawling around doesn't mean they are real or true. The next time she started feeling really stuck, Zah'Nayla practiced thinking about her ANTs crawling back down into the anthill, leaving lots and lots of space for her to do her best work.

For You to Do

Automatic negative thoughts often sound something like this: I can't do this, I always get the wrong answer, this is too hard for me, or I always forget.

Think about a time when you felt overwhelmed, worried, or nervous. Write about what happened:

_____

_____

_____

_____

_____

Now, write about one of the ANTs (automatic negative thoughts) you had during this time:

_____

_____

_____

_____

_____

Was the thought true?   Yes   No

How do you know? _____

_____

_____

_____

How helpful was your thought in the situation?

   1   2   3   4   5   6   7   8   9   10

Not helpful at all   Really helpful

When you notice a thought that might be an ANT, stop for a minute, close your eyes, and ask yourself:

Is this thought true?   Yes   No

How do I know? _____

_____

_____

_____

How much is this thought helping me?

   1   2   3   4   5   6   7   8   9   10

Not helpful at all   Really helpful

If you discover that the thought is not true or not helpful, it's an ANT, and it doesn't belong in the middle of whatever you are doing.

So, do some grounding, take some calming breaths, ride your roller coaster of feelings, or practice kindness to yourself. You might notice that as you ground and calm yourself, as you use your Mindful Me strategies, your ANTs settle down and go back into their anthill.

More to Do

Sometimes, even when you've managed to get those ANTs back into their hill, you might need a little more help to get unstuck. You can do this by giving yourself positive support. Close your eyes, and while you breathe in, say, "I am …" and breathe out while you say, "(something positive)." For example, breathe in, "I am …" and breathe out, "smart." Take a few breaths until you notice your brain and body settling down and clearing space for you become unstuck.

When You Feel Scared About an Emergency

For You to Know

Sometimes drills feel scary. Fire drills, lockdown drills, earthquake drills, tornado drills, winter storm and snow emergency dismissal drills, and emergency evacuation drills are all done to help keep kids safe. They are really important because they help kids and adults practice so that they know exactly what to do in an emergency. If schools didn't practice what to do in these situations, kids and teachers might not know what to do in a real emergency. But the drills are loud and can feel scary, especially because when they happen you might not know if it is a real emergency or just practice.

Cullen is really scared of fire drills. They're so loud, and everyone has to move really fast, and he worries he'll get left behind. Worst of all, when there's a drill, Cullen gets scared that it's a real emergency. Cullen has started to be so scared that there might be a fire drill that he cries before school. Once he gets to school, it is hard for him to pay attention.

Cullen and his mom came up with a plan for him to use the next time there was a fire drill. One day, in the middle of a math lesson, it happened. The fire alarms started ringing. Cullen followed his class to the safety spot. While he waited, he started to feel really dizzy. He looked around to find something steady, like he had discussed with his mom. He turned his attention to the huge oak tree by the baseball diamond and tuned out all the movement and noise around him. He took a deep breath and breathed in the strength and stillness of the oak tree, and breathed out calm. He breathed in strength and breathed out calm until the stillness of the tree was inside him.

Now when he thinks about fire drills or emergencies happening, he knows he has a way to feel strong and calm even in the middle of noise and movement. Knowing this makes him a lot less worried about drills.

For You to Do

Let's practice:

1. **Think**

   Think about a situation at school that feels stressful in a scary way. Notice how your body feels as you think about this thing happening.

2. **Find**

   Find something near you that is stable and strong, something that wouldn't be easy to move around.

3. **Breathe in the stillness**

   Focus your attention on the stable, strong object. Look at it, and touch it if you can. As you breathe in, say to yourself, "I am breathing in the strength and stillness of (the object)." Breathe out, saying to yourself, "I am strong and still." Make sure you breathe out twice as long as you breathe in. Do this from three to five times.

4. **Notice**

   After you have breathed in and out a few times, notice what is happening in your body. Is your heartbeat slower? Does your body feel calmer? Are your thoughts more clear and steady?

More to Do

A simple tool to remember when everything around you feels stressful is called **SLOW**ing down:

> **S**: **S**often your face, soften your eyes, soften your mouth, and slowly soften your body.

> **L**: **L**ower your shoulders.

> **O**: **O**pen your chest and your belly with three to five deep breaths.

> **W**: **W**ilt your fingers and your hands. Relax and let them go.

Take a minute to notice how your body feels.

Try it now, and if it seems helpful, use it the next time your worries start flying around.

For You to Know

Going to school can be difficult, and going to school when you are worried about leaving your family is even harder. It can feel like you're alone in a place that doesn't always seem safe. We feel worry and stress in our bodies, and we also feel safety in our bodies. One of the best ways to feel safe in your body is to get a hug—and you can get the safe feeling of a hug any time you need it if you know about butterfly hugs.

Cole didn't want to go to school. At school, he really missed his mom and dad. He felt lonely without them, and he worried that they might even forget him. Cole loved the feeling of being hugged because it helped him feel safe, and that was another hard thing about being at school—no hugs, even if he really needed one. One day, he thought maybe he could give himself a hug. He reached his arms around himself and squeezed. He closed his eyes and thought about what it felt like to be hugged. It really helped. He felt safer and less lonely. He told his dad about it that night, and his dad said, "My mom used to call those butterfly hugs. Those are really good."

For You to Do

Hugs are one of the best and fastest ways to help your body calm down. When you're alone or you're in a situation where you can't ask a trusted adult for a hug, take a couple of minutes to give yourself a butterfly hug. Here's how:

1. Sit comfortably. With your eyes closed, do grounding and take a couple of calming breaths.

2. Wrap your arms around yourself, so that each of your hands touches the back of the opposite shoulder.

3. Breathe in, and then out, feeling the warmth and weight of your arms wrapped around your body

4. Now gently squeeze your arms tighter to give yourself a bigger hug. Count 1, 2, 3, then relax your arms for a count of three, still hugging.

5. Do it again, squeezing for 1, 2, 3, then relaxing for 1, 2, 3. Do it as long as you wish.

After you do the butterfly hug, take a few moments to think about how giving yourself a hug made you feel and which part of the hug you liked the best. Write about it here, or draw a picture.

More to Do

Another way to do the butterfly hug is to alternate the squeezes, like this: Instead of squeezing your whole body, squeeze each of your shoulders separately. First gently squeeze the right shoulder 1, 2, 3, and then the left shoulder 1, 2, 3. Then, go back to the right side and then the left side. Do it as many times as you would like.

Or you could even try tapping your shoulders, instead of squeezing. First gently tap the right shoulder 1, 2, 3, and then the left shoulder 1, 2, 3. Then, go back to the right side and then the left side. Do it as many times as you would like.

After you try the different types of butterfly hugs, take a few moments to think about how each different type of hug made you feel and which type of hug you liked the best. Write about it here, or draw a picture.

Taking a Break from Worries

For You to Know

Sometimes when worries get in the way of being able to play with your friends, focus on schoolwork, or sleep, grown-ups tell you to let your worries go. But where can they go? A worry tree is somewhere to put your worries for a while so you can take a break from them and do the things you want and need to do.

For thousands of years, the worry tree has stood strong and steady. She is a grand tree with deep, strong roots and a huge trunk with branches that are as big as the legs of an elephant and leaves as strong as leather. She lives to take care of worries so you don't have to. To visit the worry tree, relax and close your eyes. Take three deep, long breaths and get ready to use your imagination.

Imagine a meadow path with flowers and tall grass on each side. The path is worn and clear from many travelers. The path enters the woods with all kinds of trees and birds singing as they fly from branch to branch. Right away you see the magnificent worry tree straight ahead. It is stronger and steadier than any of the other trees.

A sign by the worry tree reads, "Welcome to the worry tree! She loves to hold worries and keep them safe. It is her reason for being. It makes her roots grow strong and her leaves grow wide."

You walk up to the worry tree. Standing there, breathing deeply, you choose the worries you would like to leave. You pick a worry that has been on your mind a lot. You hold the worry up to the worry tree. A branch slowly reaches out to you, and two of her strong leaves gently wrap around the worry. The tree pulls the worry up into her branches, safe and sound.

You feel light and calm because your worries are safe. Now you can play with friends, take a test, or sleep. Sometimes you might want your worry back so you can think about it, feel your feelings about it, and maybe make some choices about how to handle it. If you do want your worry back, all you need to do is walk up to the worry tree and reach your hands up. The worry tree's branches will reach down and hand you your worry—safe and sound.

For You to Do

Draw a picture of the worry tree. All around her branches and leaves, write the worries you would like her to hold while you play, study, or spend time with people you love.

When you are done, notice how your body feels from your head to your toes. Notice your thoughts and your feelings. If you notice any worried thoughts or feelings, you can add them to the worry tree.

More to Do

You can use the worry tree whenever you like. You might need your worry tree at school or during a sleepover at a friend's house. You can redraw your worry tree on a piece of paper to keep at school or in your backpack. You can even use your imagination to visit her. Wherever you are, you can always hand your worries over to the worry tree and take a break.

When You Can't Sleep

For You to Know

Sometimes worries seem to feel worse at night. In the quiet, when you're lying in bed, your worries might keep your brain and body from falling asleep, even if you're really tired.

Sometimes Elise's worries are so big that she has trouble sleeping. She notices that her muscles feel tense and tight and that her body feels shaky. It seems like her heart is pounding hard and fast. Elise's dad has taught her that relaxing her body also helps relax her brain so that she can fall asleep. When Elise is tight with worry and can't sleep, she closes her eyes and starts to relax all the muscles in her body.

For You to Do

When your body is tense and your heart races with worry, you can relax your muscles bit by bit, and your relaxing body will calm your worrying mind.

You can practice relaxing your muscles either sitting in a comfortable chair or lying on your bed. Once you are comfortable:

1. Close your eyes.

2. Take a few deep, slow breaths.

3. Keep taking your slow breaths as you start to pay attention to your legs and your feet. Imagine you are standing in a mud puddle. Squish your toes deep into the mud. Try to push them all the way down to the bottom of the mud puddle. Squeeze your legs hard to push your feet, spread your toes, and try to sink down deep. Now relax your feet and relax your legs.

4. Next, pay attention to your belly. Imagine you are lying in the grass on a beautiful summer day. Squeeze your stomach muscles as tight as you can, pressing your back against the chair back or the bed. Hold them nice and tight. Keep doing your breathing. Go ahead and relax your belly.

5. Now imagine you are a turtle by a beautiful pond in the sunshine. Feel the sun on your face. Pull yourself down into your shell, pulling your shoulders up to your ears and pushing your head down to your shoulders. Squeeze tight to scrunch yourself into your turtle shell. Now relax, bringing your shoulders back down and reaching your head nice and tall. Relax in the warm sunshine.

6. Now imagine you are in the park on a spring day. A beautiful, brightly colored butterfly lands right on the tip of your nose, and its wings tickle your cheeks. Try to wiggle the butterfly off your nose by scrunching your nose and your face. Wiggle your nose. Wrinkle your face tight. When it flies away, relax your face completely.

7. Now just breathe for a while. Think about how relaxed and heavy your body feels. You started by tightening your legs and feet, and now they are relaxed. You squeezed your belly, and now it is relaxed. You scrunched your shoulders, and now they are relaxed. You scrunched your nose and face, and now they are relaxed. Your whole body is relaxed.

8. If it's bedtime, you are relaxed and ready to fall asleep. Keep your eyes closed and let yourself drift to sleep. If it's not bedtime, take another deep breath in, and when you feel ready, open your eyes.

More to Do

To fall asleep, it is important to start getting ready before you climb into bed. Here are some things you can do to help sleep come:

- Use your bed only for calm activities, like resting and sleeping.

- Turn off all your screens at least an hour before bedtime.

- Eat a healthy snack that has a good balance of carbohydrates and a little protein, like crackers and cheese, a banana or an apple with a small scoop of peanut butter, trail mix, cereal and milk, or a yogurt.

- Take a warm shower or bath.

- Have things around you that make you feel happy and safe (like a special stuffed animal or blanket).

- Do the muscle relaxation.

With your parents, plan which ones you want to try. Go ahead and circle the ones you will use. Once you try something for a few days, you can decide if it's something you'd like to keep doing to help you sleep.

When You Panic

For You to Know

Stop, refocus, breathe is a mindful coping tool that's made up of some of the tools you've already learned. It's good to use when you feel sudden panic. And when you have to face your biggest fears, having a plan can also help.

Jayden had never been on an airplane. He wanted to go on vacation, but he was really worried about flying. Jayden started to panic when he got to the airport. Suddenly, he was sweating and dizzy. He felt like he couldn't breathe. His mind was spinning with worry, and his heart felt like it was beating out of his chest. Jayden's mom sat down with him and reminded him of all of the hard work he had been doing to learn to calm his worries. Together, they calmed Jayden's panic by stopping his mind from stressed-out thinking, by refocusing, and by breathing.

Then Jayden and his mom made a plan to help him get less scared before the next time he had to fly. Starting with the things that were just a little scary, Jayden and his mom listed steps he could try to take. First, they looked at pictures of airplanes and watched airline commercials online. Any time he felt too scared to keep going, they used the stop, refocus, and breathe tool. Then they tried again. Jayden and his mom practiced talking about vacations and started planning their next vacation together. Again, any time he felt too scared to keep going, they used the stop, refocus, and breathe tool, then tried again.

Jayden gained skills and confidence. They took the next big step and went to an airport to practice using the tools around real airplanes. Last, when he was feeling ready, they used Jayden's new Mindful Me tools while they took their next vacation. Jayden was able to get on the plane and fly. He felt a little scared, only this time it was not too bad because he had practiced and he knew he could do it.

For You to Do

Here's how to use the stop, refocus, and breathe tool:

1. **Stop**

   As soon as you feel worry in your body (see activity 2), say "Stop" inside your head. This reminds your brain to stop thinking about your worry.

2. **Refocus**

   Pay attention to what is happening right now. When you focus on what you see, hear, smell, feel, and taste (see activity 9), it gives your mind something to pay attention to that *isn't* your worried, panicky thoughts.

3. **Breathe**

   Breathe in, saying to yourself, "I am breathing in for one count … one." Breathe out, saying to yourself, "I am breathing out for two counts … one … two." Do this four times (see activity 1). Repeat as many times as you need to until you notice that you are calming down.

More to Do

Many times, it's best to plan what we'll do with our biggest fears before they come up and cause us to panic, like Jayden and his mom did. The steps that follow will guide you in creating your plan. You can also download a blank copy at http://www. newharbinger.com/41313 to make a new plan.

Think about something you don't want to do, because it feels really scary. Write it down here:

_____

_____

_____

_____

Now, try to think about little steps you could take to slowly get used to that big scary thing. A grown-up can help you think of steps. After you list the steps you can think of, put a number next to each step that stands for how scary it is: 1 = Not at all scary, 2 = Just a little scary, 3 = Kind of scary, 4 = Pretty scary, and 5 = Really scary.

Write your list and put how scary each is. Now, starting with the things that are just a little scary (the 2s), create a plan for trying each step you listed.

Step	How scary is it?

Any time you try a step and feel too scared to keep going, use the stop, refocus, and breathe tool. Then try again.

Having an Attitude of Gratitude

For You to Know

Having *gratitude* means being thankful. Doctors and others who study stress and happiness have figured out that being thankful can help you fight stress and feel happy. When you practice being thankful every day, it is called a *gratitude practice*. It is something that a lot of people have learned to do to live a happier, calmer life.

For the last year, Ben has had a gratitude practice that he uses in the morning, whenever he feels upset, and in the evening. He practices being grateful in three ways.

On his way to school each morning, Ben looks for three things he is thankful for. Last Tuesday, for example, he decided he was grateful for the bluebird in his front yard, his own soccer ball, and the lunch he was taking to school. Just thinking about those good things helped him feel happy as he started his day.

When he gets upset, Ben uses the alphabet to focus on good stuff. He thinks about the letter A until he comes up with something he is thankful for that begins with A (like anime, or August, when there's no school). Then he goes to the letter B and does the same (basketball maybe, or burgers). He goes through the alphabet until he is feeling better.

The third part of his gratitude practice is a journal he writes in at night. Before he goes to sleep, he writes down one thing he is grateful for learning that day. First, he says thanks to himself for trying hard, and then he takes time be thankful for the things he has learned that helped him that day.

For You to Do

Next time you go to school, notice three things you feel thankful for. When you come home, write or draw about them here.

Do it for four more days. On a separate paper, write down what you notice each day.

You can continue to do this every day. Once you get used to practicing gratitude, you don't need to write the three things down.

More to Do

Try practicing gratitude using the ABCs. In the blank space, write or draw a picture of something you feel thankful for, beginning with each letter. Continue going through the alphabet until you are feeling better.

You can also use the letters of your name. Ben thought about baseball for the letter *B*, elephants for the letter *E*, and how good it feels to have no homework for the letter *N*.

For You to Know

You have learned a lot about how to use mindfulness tools to calm your worries. But even with all you know, you probably still have times when you are like the Stressed-Out Me and times when you are like the Mindful Me. Everyone does—we all have both parts. The more you practice mindfulness tools, the stronger your Mindful Me becomes.

For You to Do

Through your thoughts and actions, you can feed either your Stressed-Out Me or your Mindful Me. Take some time to go through this whole workbook and look at all the tools you've learned to use. For each one you like (and that feeds your Mindful Me), put a check mark next to it here. If you want your Mindful Me to be super strong, feed it with lots of practice.

☐ Using your Mindful Me action guides   ☐ Learning to listen and talk

☐ Asking for help   ☐ Practicing compassion

☐ Grounding and calming breaths   ☐ Choosing who to spend time with

☐ Watching for your Stressed-Out Me   ☐ Planning ahead to deal with stress

☐ The mind jar   ☐ Getting unstuck

☐ Attention with your five senses   ☐ Staying calm during an emergency

☐ The sky story   ☐ Butterfly hugs

☐ Practicing curiosity   ☐ Taking a break with the worry tree

☐ Remembering your mindful why   ☐ Relaxing your muscles to help you
                                              sleep
☐ Heartfulness
                                            ☐ Stop, refocus, breathe
☐ Your peaceful place
                                            ☐ An attitude of gratitude
☐ Riding the roller coaster of feelings

☐ Mindful creating

More to Do

Any time you use any of your Mindful Me action guides you are feeding your Mindful Me. Which ones have you used? Put a check mark next to each. Which ones would you like to practice more? Draw a food next to it to help you remember that you are feeding your Mindful Me each time you use it. Erica loves pizza, so she drew a pizza next to "I am right here, right now." Because she has never tasted a star fruit, she chose that for "I am curious. I can try." She chose a beautiful cake for "I choose my actions on purpose" because she wants to be a wonderful baker someday (her mindful why), and she knows her mindfulness tools will help her get there. What are your favorites?

- ☐ I am right here, right now.

- ☐ I am mindfully aware inside and out.

- ☐ I can choose and maintain my focus.

- ☐ I am curious. I can try.

- ☐ I use my mindfulness tools to cope.

- ☐ I choose my actions on purpose.

- ☐ I am kind and caring to myself and others.

Still More to Do

You have worked really hard to use your Mindful Me throughout this workbook, but when your Stressed-Out Me gets really big and loud, it can be hard to remember what you've learned to do to help calm down. This is why it's good to keep a calm-down kit with you. A calm-down kit is a place for you to gather all the tools you have found that help your worries feel better.

To make one, start by finding an empty box, like a shoebox, or maybe even the Practicing Attention box you used (see activity 9). You might decide to decorate your box, but you don't have to. Although you have learned so many new things throughout this workbook, there might be other tools you would like to put in your kit. Choose things that you can touch, smell, and look at that help you feel calm and use your mindfulness tools. Here are some ideas:

Things that feel good to touch, smell, hear, and feel:	Things that help focus your attention:	Things that help you use deep breathing:
• Squeeze toys • Textured balls • Piece of fleece or a little plush toy • Your mind jar • Play-doh • Lotion	• Books • Coloring and activity books and colored pencils or crayons • Puzzle books and pencils	• Bubbles • Pinwheel

What else will you add to your calm-down kit?

_____

_____

_____

_____

_____

Finally, put your calm-down kit in or near your peaceful place (see activity 16), so you can use it there when you need to.

For You to Know

All kids have worries. Some worries you can handle on your own. Sometimes, though, things can happen in your life that are very scary or feel too big to handle. These bigger things are more than a stressful test at school or a friend who said a mean thing.

If something like this has happened to you, you may have gone through what doctors call *trauma*. When you think about these types of worries, you may think, "I'm not sure what to do to feel okay," or "I don't know how to handle this on my own."

It's okay if you feel overwhelmed or are not sure what to do. Have you ever felt that way? Anna has.

Anna's parents got into a big fight. They were both yelling, a lot. She was upstairs, and she heard loud noises like pans crashing in the kitchen. She was really scared and did not know what do to. She could feel her heart pounding, and she was working very hard not to cry. She wasn't sure why. Her mom had always told her it was okay to cry, even good to cry sometimes. When Anna finally started to cry, she felt like she could not stop. She felt very overwhelmed and was not sure what she was feeling or thinking. She was all by herself for a while.

Later that night, Anna and her mom left to go to her grandmother's house, and Anna felt confused.

What kinds of things can feel this way? Doctors who study trauma tell us that there are two types: *Big T Trauma* and *little t trauma*. Big T Trauma is something that happens that most people would agree is very scary, like an earthquake, a bad car accident in which you get hurt, or the sudden loss of someone you love.

Little t trauma is something that happens to you personally that is really hard for you to handle—for example, the loss of a pet or your parents getting a divorce. These events can also feel bigger than your ability to cope with them.

Both types of trauma can really stress kids out. If you have been through a trauma—whether Big T or little t—you may feel okay. You may be relieved that the traumatic event has passed. But sometimes trauma can affect you for a long time after it happens, so notice your body, your feelings, and what you are thinking. If the thoughts and feelings all feel really big and you want help, ask for it. There is help for you.

For You to Do

Not all scary things are trauma, but some are. You can tell it was trauma if when it happened you felt:

1. truly scared that you or someone you love might not be okay,

2. completely overwhelmed and struggled to know what to think, feel, or do,

or

3. weren't sure if anyone or anything could help at that time.

You might have felt stuck or frozen (like you could not move). You might have wanted to run away or fight somebody. You might have felt faint or like you were going to pass out. You might have felt your heart beating really fast. There are many different ways a person might feel during a traumatic event.

If you like, write or draw a picture about any time you can remember when you felt one of those ways. It's okay if you have a lot of things to write or draw (you can use as much extra paper as you need!) and it's okay if you can't think of any.

More to Do

You might be feeling a lot, nothing, or a medium amount of stress or anxiety after doing this activity. All kids are different. Sometimes kids feel a lot after talking or writing about an event. It is a good idea to check in with your feelings. These feelings scales can help you know when it might be a good idea to use your grounding and calming breaths and when you might want to ask for support.

Circle the number on this scale that shows how much stress or anxiety you are feeling right now.

1	2	3	4	5	6	7	8	9	10

I am doing okay.   I feel a little   I feel a lot of
                                  stressed/anxious.   stress/anxiety.

Sometimes kids are aware of their feelings, and sometimes they feel numb, as if they had no feelings. How numb are you right now?

1	2	3	4	5	6	7	8	9	10

I am feeling   I feel a little numb.   I feel totally
my feelings.   numb.

If you circled 4 or above on either scale, it a good idea to use your grounding and calming breaths tools. If you are feeling a lot of anxiety or numbness (from 5 to 10), share how you are feeling with your parent or an adult you trust. Talking about these big feelings and events can be hard. You did a lot of good and difficult work here!

Being Trauma Informed
What Does PTSD Feel Like?

For You to Know

Sometimes kids who have been through trauma have trouble not thinking about it. They feel like it is happening right now, even though it is not. They have nightmares and are super jumpy and anxious. Doctors call this post-traumatic stress disorder, or PTSD.

This happened to Anna. Even though her parents were not fighting anymore, she kept thinking about their big fight and more.

It has been a year since Anna's parents got into their big fight, and Anna still feels jumpy whenever she hears loud sounds, like pots and pans crashing. Anna feels a lot of stress and anxiety in her belly and chest when people raise their voices. This feels like stomachaches, and sometimes her chest feels tight and heavy like she can't breathe. She keeps having nightmares about that night. Worse, she thinks about that night when she is with her friends or doing homework, and she feels like she can't focus on anything but that. She worries about her parents all the time because she loves them both a lot.

Anna decided to tell her mom how she was feeling. Her mom gave her a hug and made an appointment for Anna to talk to a really nice counselor who helped her handle her overwhelming thoughts and feelings. Anna learned ways to handle her memories and feelings so she could play with her friends and do her homework without all the worries getting in the way.

For You to Do

Think about the last activity and the stressful things you wrote about or drew. Circle any statements that reflect how this event feels to you *now*. It is okay if you circle a lot, and it is okay if you don't feel or notice any of these things.

Things you might notice in your body:

- I feel like I can't control how I respond to stress or worries.

- I feel sick a lot of the time, and it is hard for me to get better.

- I wish I did not have to be in my body.

- I feel anxiety and worry in my body all the time.

- My body feels either really sleepy and heavy or really tense and wound up.

- I can't sleep or I want to sleep all the time.

Things you might notice in your thinking:

- I have difficulty thinking, learning, and focusing.

- I have trouble remembering things.

- I have trouble switching from one thought to another.

- I keep thinking of things that have happened.

Things you might notice in your feelings:

- I don't feel like I am that good at anything or good for anything.

- I feel unsafe.

- I have trouble handling my emotions.

- I have trouble feeling close to people and trusting them.

- I have trouble making friends.

- I feel sad and worried all the time.

- I have trouble feeling anything at all.

- My feelings feel too big.

Things you might notice in your actions:

- I do things without thinking.

- When I play, it is not fun like before or other kids think I am weird.

- I keep getting into fights even though I don't mean to.

- I make bad choices.

- I have tried to hurt myself.

- I have trouble doing the things I am supposed to do.

- I don't do fun things like I used to.

If the trauma that happened feels really big, and you notice a lot of things in your body, thoughts, feelings, and actions, it is probably a good idea to get more support.

Mindfulness for Anxious Kids

First, give yourself a lot of thankfulness for being willing to think, talk, and write about really hard things that have happened in your life.

Second, check one of these boxes:

☐ What has happened in my life feels really big. I have noticed a lot of things in my body, feelings, thoughts, and actions that are related to what happened. I am going to tell a parent or an adult I trust about this.

☐ I am not sure. I am going to show a parent or an adult I trust my work on this activity, and we can figure this out together.

☐ I know what to do: (1) I already have talked to my parents or someone I trust about this, or (2) what happened was scary but I don't think about it much and I know I am safe, or (3) what happened was scary and I have lots of tools to help myself calm down and people to support me.

☐ Something else (write here): _____

_____

_____

More to Do

Check in with your feelings again. It's okay if you are feeling a lot, nothing, or a medium amount of stress or anxiety after doing this activity. Once you check in with your feelings, you can tell an adult you trust how you are feeling. You can talk about PTSD and how much support you might want right now.

Circle the number on this scale that shows how much stress or anxiety you are feeling right now.

1	2	3	4	5	6	7	8	9	10

I am doing okay.   I feel a little   I feel a lot of
                                     stressed/anxious.   stress/anxiety.

Sometimes kids are aware of their feelings, and sometimes they feel numb, as if they had no feelings. How numb are you right now?

1	2	3	4	5	6	7	8	9	10

I am feeling   I feel a little numb.   I feel totally
my feelings.   numb.

When your body, thoughts, feelings, and actions are all affected by what has happened in your life, it is definitely time to talk to an adult you trust.

Write down the names of three people who would be safe adults to tell about your experiences and how you are feeling now.

1. _____

2. _____

3. _____

How could you let them know you'd like to talk? Choose one or two of these ideas, and use the blank lines to add some of your own.

- I can find a quiet time and tell a parent that I have something important to talk about.

- I can write a letter or note to an adult I trust and say that I want to talk.

- I can call or text an adult I trust and say I have something important I want to talk about.

- If I am nervous, I can have a friend go with me to the schools counselor's office and ask for an appointment.

- I can tell my teacher (or coach, doctor, or my friend's big sister) that something is bothering me and I need help finding someone safe to talk to.

Write your ideas here: _____

_____

_____

_____

Still More to Do

When you are ready to talk, you can tell the person you are talking to about what you have been noticing in your body, thoughts, feelings, and actions. If you feel like you need more support, go to the next person on your list. Keep going until you find someone safe who can listen and support you.

Last, go back through this book and practice your Mindful Me tools to help calm your body, settle your thoughts, cope with your stress and big feelings, and make the best choices for you. It might take some hard work and a lot of support, but your Mindful Me knows that you are worth the effort!

Acknowledgments

We would like to acknowledge Wendy Millstine at New Harbinger Publications for helping us form and mold a book around our Mindful Me concept. Also, we have overwhelming gratitude for Elizabeth Hollis-Hansen and Clancy Drake, who so carefully edited this book to be sure it spoke to children and adults in a way that everyone could hear. Last, thank you, New Harbinger Publications, for believing in our Mindful Me, too!

Catherine Cook-Cottone, PhD, is full professor at the University at Buffalo, State University of New York; as well as a practicing psychologist. She has written two books on mindfulness and yoga for self-regulation—one for mental health professionals and one for school personnel. Cook-Cottone is on the scientific program committee for the Symposium on Yoga Research, and a consultant to the United Nations Foundation, UNICEF, and Africa Yoga Project. She is founder and president of Yogis in Service, Inc.

Rebecca K. Vujnovic, PhD, is clinical associate professor at the University at Buffalo, State University of New York; as well as program director for the school of psychology's MA program. In addition, Vujnovic maintains a small private practice, specifically working with children using mindfulness techniques to manage anxiety, stress, and worry.

Foreword writer **Christopher Willard, PsyD**, is a psychologist and educational consultant based in Boston, MA, specializing in mindfulness. He has been practicing meditation for twenty years, and leads mindfulness and mental health workshops internationally. He currently serves on the board of directors at the Institute for Meditation and Psychotherapy, and is president of thef Mindfulness in Education Network. He has presented at TEDx conferences, and his thoughts have appeared in *The New York Times, The Washington Post,* www.mindful.org, and elsewhere. He is author of *Child's Mind, Growing Up Mindful, Raising Resilience,* and three other books. He teaches at Harvard Medical School.

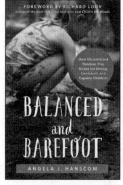

Register your **new harbinger** titles for additional benefits!

When you register your **new harbinger** title—purchased in any format, from any source—you get access to benefits like the following:

- Downloadable accessories like printable worksheets and extra content

- Instructional videos and audio files

- Information about updates, corrections, and new editions

Not every title has accessories, but we're adding new material all the time.

Access free accessories in 3 easy steps:

1. Sign in at NewHarbinger.com (or **register** to create an account).

2. Click on **register a book**. Search for your title and click the **register** button when it appears.

3. Click on the **book cover or title** to go to its details page. Click on **accessories** to view and access files.

That's all there is to it!

If you need help, visit:

NewHarbinger.com/accessories

new harbinger
CELEBRATING
40 YEARS